Margaret J Swinney
1351 Creace St
1351 Creace St Pa
Pa
For Miss C

Our Children in Heaven.

TO THOSE

WHO HAVE BEEN BEREAVED OF THEIR CHILDREN

CONTENTS.

CHAPTER VIII.

CHAPTER IX.

CHAPTER X.

PREFACE.

The earliest hour of the summer mornings was devoted to the composition of this little book.

The time was one of approaching lights and receding shadows.

It is now the same hour in the moral world: and my subject is illumined with a touch of that Morning which cometh after the Night.

I publish it:

Hoping to alleviate the sorrows of others by some thoughts which were suggested by my own:

Hoping also to lead the mind of my reader, by little things and through quiet paths, to a recognition of the Highest Truth yet revealed to man.

THE AUTHOR.

NEW ORLEANS, LA.

Our Children in Heaven.

CHAPTER I.

IS THERE NO LIGHT?

WE meet with few circumstances in life so painful, so bewildering, so crushing as the death of a little child. It is painful to the sensibilities; bewildering to the understanding; crushing to the heart. The whole man is wounded by the blow.

There is nothing which so seems to violate the order, the beauty, we may say, the sanctity of nature and the laws of Heaven, as the sickness and suffering of a little child.

How tenderly the interest of the whole house centres in the chamber of such a patient! There are no pattering feet in the hall; no busy little hands in the corners; no merry voices on the stairway; no wild shouts in the garden. The playroom is shut up; the books and the toys are put away. The parlor is dark and silent: who cares for social life now?

Every one steps lightly and talks softly. The neighbors inquire at the door and turn gently away. No little playmates are admitted, not even the sunbeams; the room is darkened. Unteased, unpetted, the little dog cowers under the chair; the kitten dozes on the rug. Even the canary does not sing. The house is very, very quiet. Foreboding, that spiritual cloud, impends over all.

The darling of the parent's heart, the centre now of all thoughts and fears and prayers, turns uneasily on a bed of anguish. The golden curls are tangled in the tossings. The sleepless eyes are bloodshot with fever; the cheek burns; the brow aches; the little heart struggles like a frightened bird. All is wrong. The delicate machinery of those wonderful organs, bound together in the body in a sacred brotherhood of uses, is out of order. The evil spirits of discord and pain are holding carnival in the seething blood and the tortured nerves. How piteous, how revolting!

And the victim? Some patient, helpless, little creature, ignorant of sin, innocent of wrong. A few days ago blooming and happy, peering forth with loving eyes and heavenly greetings into the great dark world before it. Now, a little Isaac bound upon the altar of sacrifice; no ram in the thicket, no rescuing angel in the sky!

At the sight of such cruel violence, such terrible injustice, we are ready to exclaim with the Roman Governor, as he turned from the celestial face of Jesus to the fiercely-accusing and malignant Jews:

"Why, what evil hath he done?"

The machinery of our cosmic Nature is sometimes ajar also. She has her earthquakes, her storms, her floods, her fires, emblematic of the grandest and darkest experiences of the human soul. Has she not also some horrible distortions in her tinier realm to correspond with the suffering and death of children? Is there any exception to the ubiquity and the tyranny of Evil? Do not death and sorrow and rapine and wrong ravage also the infant realms of her shining kingdoms? Do not her fay souls consume in the sunbeams, and her fairies perish in the meadows? Are there not voices of anguish and terror, which we cannot interpret, in the sounds of her winds and her waters?

Days and nights of racking disease in the body of the little patient—days and nights of corroding anxiety in the hearts of the watchers! Oh, the struggle betwixt fear and hope! the exultation of one day, the despair of the next! These are the experiences of life; these are the watchings, which give a "sober coloring" to all things afterwards; which bring "the faith that looks through death," and such tenderness of heart, that

> "——— The meanest flower that blows can give
> Thoughts that do often lie too deep for tears."

The house grows more quiet than ever; almost a desolation. The wearied, loving nurses move ghost-like to and fro. A little light shines through the shutters all night long. The doctors come and go, eagerly expected, long delayed at the door with anxious questionings. The shadow deepens over all hearts. The shadow deepens also over the little stream of life, near which the loving ones are watching. 'Tis the shadow of the Great Abyss which it slowly approaches.

And now the brain is confused; the little mind wanders; the child is delirious.

Have you ever watched the delirium of a little child? The most pitiful, painful, harrowing thing in all the phenomena of disease! What gentle Tassos talking to angels in their gloomy prisons, what pure Ophelias weaving their garlands of song and madness, ever melted the soul into such agony as those "sweet bells, jangled and out of tune," the dying thoughts of little children?

The doctor has ordered a warm bath. The little fellow's own bath-tub is brought to the bed-side, in which he has so often splashed with delight, rosy-faced and laughing-eyed between his shower of overhanging curls. The eager, heart-aching, and trembling mother prepares him for the bath, with gushing, tender, baby words reminding him of his old delights, and promising him such a happy time. Alas! it is all changed now. The busy demon of disease has defaced the texture and marred the delicate workings of that little brain. The child listens to nothing; remembers nothing; understands nothing. All is blurred, distorted, and magnified. He gazes at the water in bewilderment, screams and clings in terror to his mother's knees.

"Oh, mamma, mamma! please—please do not throw me into the big river."

She lifts him back into the bed, kisses his forehead, and sinks weeping at his feet.

The little girl calls wildly and eagerly for her papa. He rushes to her side, kisses her cheek, strokes her hair, raises her sweet little hand to his lips, addressing her by all the tender names in which love's vocabulary is so rich; but all in vain. She shrinks from him; she does not know him.

"I want my own papa. You are not my papa. My papa is not an old man with a long gray beard. No, no, no! I want my own papa."

Then sinking back, she folds her tiny hands meekly together, and looking upwards, like the pictures of the little Samuel praying, she strangely mingles the sweet words of the Lord's prayer with disjointed ideas of her playmates, her dolls, and her little flower-garden.

Ah! don't you see there is no hope? The Angel of Death stands there invisible, quietly unraveling the tangled web of life, intending to take all that is beautiful and spiritual in it away with himself.

Do you remember having ever seen little children a short while before they sickened and died, playing in a graveyard on a bright, summer day? You will recall something strange and beautiful in their conduct, for "coming events cast their shadows before." They seemed in love with the spot, flitting about like sunbeams from one little grave to another, joyously but softly and tenderly. They were fascinated with the sculptured angels and the sleeping infants and the white lambs, and the vases and wreaths of flowers, and all the charming little mementoes of the "vanished hands" and "the voices that are still." They were loath to go away, as if attracted by the sphere of hundreds of invisible and happy little spirits. They evidently thought that death and burial were pleasant and lovely things; and that it would be delightful to lay their own little bodies under the soft green turf, and live evermore in that "happy land, far, far away," of which they were accustomed to sing so sweetly.

Oh, how sweet, how painful and sweet it is to stoop and bend, day after day, with weary care over the common dust-heap of our past experiences, and humming old tunes to ourselves, and thinking of our lost hopes and buried loves, to pick out the little diamonds of memory and put them into our bosoms!

A strange time is it from midnight to cock-crowing—a dark, sad, silent, fearful time, when evil spirits and evil men are abroad; when the world lies cold and dim, and the heavens are afar off; the time for murders, and thefts, and ghost-walkings, and for strange and secret crimes; and especially the time for pestilence to strike and for death to seize. The temperature of the earth declines rapidly, and darkness, that hateful thing, reaches its climax. The night-dews come out everywhere like cold drops upon nature's brow.

Then it is the great cry is made, "the bridegroom cometh!"

Then it is the human spirit lays its heavy burden down, and sleeps, to experience "another morn than ours."

Then it is we hear the wild shrieks of the bereaved Rachels, refusing to be comforted.

After midnight the vital current grows sluggish and shallow, soon to disappear among the quicksands of death. The eyes become dim; and oh, fearful change! the soul-light fades from the face. The nearest watcher suddenly whispers, "dead;" the father inquires tremulously, "dead?" the kneeling mother shrieks wildly, "dead!" The pent-up anguish of all hearts now bursts out into loud wails of grief. The doors are opened; the house is awakened; there is anxious running to and fro; and all is movement and bustle where everything was lately so fearfully still. In the midst of it all, a strange, calm, luminous halo seems to settle down upon the little corpse, as if the invisible God had waved his hands in blessing over the face of the dead child.

Yes! there lies the Deserted House. It was

builded of the earth, and has fallen again to the ground. Life and Thought have gone away, side by side. All is dark within. No light in the window; no murmur at the door. No more of mirth or merry-making sound. All is naked, vacant, deserted. Close the shutters; close the door. Come away! come away!

Ah, Poet! thou hast done well.

Thou too, Artist! hast sweetly echoed the Poet's thought. See that long, low couch in the silent room, bearing the still form, covered with a snow-white cloth. The little lute with its broken string has fallen to the floor. There are lovers who kiss by the wall; but they are statues of cold marble. A terraced garden is seen through the doorway; but it has no living presence. Out through the arched window the angels of Life and Thought have receded into the far sunlight. How still! how cold! This is not sleep, but his brother, Death!

This is beautiful, and it is true; but it is not all. It is not half the truth. It is little; it is nothing. In the white presence of this precious little body, which will never open its enchanting eyes nor lift its beautiful hand again, we feel that Art can never utter the incommunicable sorrows of the soul.

It is the reflection of Vesuvius on the moon-lit bay of Naples, as Richter has said, in comparison with that Vesuvius which burned into the heart in the buried chambers of Pompeii.

Confronted thus with death in its least accountable form, we stand bewildered with the mystery of Life; and "obstinate questionings" about God and Spirit and Time and Immortality flow through our souls, like the night-ripples of forlorn rivers struggling eastward in the dark.

There is no separation in nature attended with such a sense of abrupt departure, absence, distance, utter and eternal abstraction, as that of friend from friend at the bed of death. All other farewells have images that fade on the sight, or echoes that die on the ear. But in this there is no trace, or token, or footprint, or sound, or shadow, which can even suggest to us which way our Beloved One has gone. At one moment we are gazing in at the windows of heaven, which lead through spiritual realms of affection and thought, all the way up to the great Source of life: the next, the windows are closed, and we are confronting dead nature alone; and the dust that is left of our friend has no more genuine connection with him than if it were a statue or a flower.

The bank of the mystical Jordan which separates the wilderness of this life from the Canaan of a better, is rimmed with total darkness. Our dear ones approach the dreaded verge and disappear from our sight. We peer in vain into the terrible abyss. The sensation is perhaps the same to them that it is to us. To their reverted eyes we may seem also to have been swallowed up in sudden night. An immeasurable wall of blackness divides us. Cries, calls, prayers, however importunate and heart-breaking from one party to the other, strike back only in wailing echoes upon themselves.

Why is this? Was it always so? Will it always be so? With uplifted hands and eager voices and aching hearts, we cry to the heavens—Is there no Light?

From the stand-points of the old Theology all is darkness. Notwithstanding the visions of poets, the speculations of philosophers, the achievements of science and reason, the ecstasies of prophet and seer, the wisdom of churches, and the light of Revelation, the life after death is as much a mystery as ever. The Apostolic Church declares that the Gospel has brought life and immortality to light; but its dim intimations teach us as little of the great Hereafter, as the murmurs of the ocean-shell tell us of the Sea. What can its foremost and wisest man show us of the whereabouts of this little departed spirit? of its present form and nature? of its habitat and surroundings? of its associates and occupations? of its mode of living and means of development?

The Word of God, so perfect in its moral law, so wonderful in its letter, so heavenly in its spirit, makes no specific and detailed revelations of the state of man after death. Its dealings, so far as it has yet been made clear to us, are with the relations between God and the human soul. "Eye hath not seen, ear hath not heard," are the words of the Prophet repeated by the Apostle, exalting hope by their vague sublimity, but stifling imagination at its birth.

Neither those who were sent from the other world to this, nor those whose spiritual eyes were opened from this world into the other, have paused from their high missions to gratify the yearning curiosity of the human heart, and to answer those children's questions, springing from our intuitive thirst for the spiritual knowledge we most need, and before which the sages of all countries are silent.

Moses and Elias, conversing with our Lord on

the Mount, let fall no secrets of their glorious dwelling-place into the eager ears of the astonished disciples. Lazarus, recalled after four days from the spiritual world, has as little to say as if he had only been awakened from a deep sleep. Those who "came out of their graves" during the wonderful commotions which followed the death and resurrection of Christ, told no tales or left no records of their supernatural experiences.

The eloquent Paul, descending from the third heaven, eloquent no longer, declares that the things heard and seen were incommunicable to man.

And John the Beloved, the Celestial, displaying his apocalyptic scroll, overwhelms us with his gorgeous visions of the Holy City, with its golden streets, and gates of pearl, and rivers of life; but we cannot see the forms of our little ones in his great multitudes, "which no man can number;" nor detect their little voices amid the stupendous sounds of the "many waters" and the "mighty thunderings," and the never-ending "Alleluias."

The Delectable Mountains of the old faith are too cold and far. From our valley of humiliation we sometimes catch glimpses of them, shining in the light of God, with awful, inaccessible serenity;

but frequently, very frequently, their forms are distorted by mists of doubt or hidden by clouds of despair. We need some great spiritual telescope to bring them near to us in all their beautiful reality. We yearn to see their green slopes and their golden valleys; their radiant domes and their happy people. Is it impossible?

This is the great spiritual want of the century, overshadowing all others. A clear, consistent, philosophical, authorized revelation of the life after death. No additions to the Word of God, but an interior view of its structure, so that the relation between the letter and the spirit shall be rationally unfolded. Statements of the facts and phenomena of the spiritual world, embodying a true psychology, free from theoretical phantasies, and solving the vexed question of the connection between mind and matter. In short, a revelation to explain the Revelation, to open the seal, to render it practical and perfect—including the grounds and laws of its own appearance, and the reasons why it was not made before, and why it is not now made in some other manner.

The heart of the Christian Church yearns after these.things, as its ideal of a perfected and crowned Christianity to reign upon the earth for ever This would indeed rescue it from its gradual disintegration, give it the creative power and glory of heavenly light, and save the world from practical infidelity, which is Death, the rider of the Pale Horse, after whom follows Hell. But the brain of the Christian Church has not been taught to expect this great thing, but rather not to expect it; to expect nothing, indeed, but the dissolution of the physical universe in elemental fire. Stupendous mistake! There are errors so vast and all-pervading in their influence on the human mind, that only individuals can be emancipated from their thraldom. They rule with a rod of iron over nations and churches and races, and only wither and die down during the weary length of suffering and darkened ages.

The bereaved mother kneels by the dead body of her child, chafing its hands, stroking its hair, calling it pet names, showering sudden kisses unreturned on its little cold face. In the presence of such imperious woe, the true friend does not reason: he weeps.

Now mark the inquiries which her affections put to her understanding—the yearning, intuitive, importunate cries for light, which a religion calling itself a revealed religion ought to stand ready to answer: Where is my child? What form has he? Is he really living? Does he see, feel, hear, think, and move as before? Who have taken charge of him? What are they doing with him? What is he doing himself? Is he satisfied? Why can I not see him and commune with him? Why was he taken?

A loving mother, bereft of her innocent offspring by the terrible agencies of evil and death, has an inalienable right to ask these questions, and to have them answered. She has a right also to measure the truthfulness and credibility of a church by its capability of answering these questions. Blind herself, she may wisely refuse to be led by the blind. God designed that the answers to these natural and proper questions should be in every mouth, should shine like sunbeams into every heart. The world knew them once; the church understood them. Like innocence and peace and goodness and all the glories of Eden, these beautiful answers have been lost—lost and forgotten. They do not even return in dreams.

Why were they lost? Why are they not restored?

Is any aching heart ever satisfied with the commonplaces of theological condolence? "The Lord gave, and the Lord hath taken away," is not an infallible quietus to our wounded affections and our revolted reason. We are not satisfied with blessings which come in the disguise of painful and fearful calamities. Our minds are confused with the ascription of all things, both good and evil, to the same omnipotent Providence. We are overwhelmed with its mysterious ways and inscrutable designs and unfathomable perplexities. And when we fail to derive any light or comfort from the teachings of the church, after honest and prayerful strivings, we are not willing to believe that the sole cause of our blindness is the unregenerate state of our own hearts.

What good does it do us to be told that our beloved child is now a disembodied spirit about the throne of God, engaged, as the angels are supposed always to be, in ecstatic contemplation of the Divine perfections? Or that she sleeps in the cold, cold ground under the watchful eyes of guardian angels, until the great trumpet shall wake her from the dead?

How long are we to be fed on husks? Is there not bread enough in our Father's house, and to spare?

Suppose an Angel of Light were suddenly to

appear, divinely commissioned, at the side of the grieving mother, illumining her vision with his radiant presence, and showering upon her the great, white calm which is the atmosphere of the celestial country. Suppose he were to take her by the hand, and with ineffable tenderness of spirit and beauty of illustration, to exhibit in the sacred light of truth itself, the exact state, present and prospective, of the little soul which has just escaped from its earthly body.

How sweet to follow the little sunbeam away into heaven, its real home! away from the cloud it has left behind it so dark and cold! from the little cloud which it here illumined with ethereal beauty!

He explains to her the nature of death, which is the resurrection. He shows her the beautiful spiritual body rising out of its natural form, in which it was imbedded during the short, happy time it lived with us. He tells her that her little one is still in the glorious human form, the image of God; and still sees, hears, feels, walks, eats, sleeps, grows; is clothed and taught, loves and is loved, all just as before—yesterday and to-morrow being the same. The life to come is a continuation of this life, as a flower is a continuation of the stem.

He shows her what heaven is and where it is; who the Lord is and where He is; by whom and how her child is received and cared for. He describes the realities of heaven; not only its prayers and hymnings, but the palaces, the gardens, the lawns, the light, the music, the lessons, the teachers, the companions, the amusements, the peace, the love, the beauty, the everyday life and business of heaven. He speaks thus, not from speculation, but experience: "as one having authority, and not as the scribes."

His great, calm, sweet words fall upon her heart like music; like the harp of David on the spirit of Saul. They shine into her understanding like light falling into prison glooms unvisited by the sun. She is born into a new world of thought and feeling. This vast, sustaining, illuminating power of direct revelation does not crush or change the natural affections. It softens and elevates and purifies and spiritualizes them. The tears she sheds are as many as before, but not so bitter. The sadness of earthly memories is henceforth lightened by a sweet, over-brooding sense of the reality and proximity of a happy spiritual world. Her heart will still ache, with that aching which knows no cure but reunion, for she is bereaved of her child;

but she will no longer murmur or rebel. She will do like David, when the servants told him his child was dead:

"And he arose from the earth and washed himself, and changed his apparel, and went into the house of the Lord and worshiped."

Just what we suppose the Lord to have done in this case by the special ministry of an angel, He has now done for the church and the world. The fulness of time has come, when the mysteries of the kingdom need no longer be clothed in parables and shrouded in "dark sayings of old." The "opening of the heavens" promised by the Lord himself is upon us. The air of the world is tremulous with ancestral voices prophesying change. The heart of humanity is expectant. A new Era of Science and Development, exclaims the philosopher! The "New Heavens and the New Earth," whispers the Christian. Some say, "Lo! here!"—others, "Lo! there!"

Meanwhile the great event, with which the womb of time had been pregnant, takes place. It comes in a manner unexpected by all men, and is not recognized. Some, like Herod, would stifle the young child at once. Some mock; most are indifferent; a few believe. The High Priests and Scribes and all the old Oracles move on as before, unconscious that their systems and philosophies are death-stricken. The light has come. But the blind will not see it: for do not all things move in circles, and the old facts perpetually recur?

"The Light shineth in darkness, and the darkness comprehended it not."

A new intercourse between the spiritual and natural worlds has been established. The heavens have been opened: the spiritual sense of the Sacred Scriptures revealed: the foundation of a new and everlasting Church has been laid. The true nature of the human soul and of its connection with the human body and with attendant spirits, that grand Psychology for which the heart of man has yearned for so many ages, is now unfolded. The laws and phenomena of the world of spirits, of heaven and hell, the veritable facts, and, as it were, the manners and customs of the life after death, have been clearly made known. The children's questions are answered. Science and Philosophy are satisfied: the Bible is vindicated: the Light has come!

When and where and by whom was this stupendous Revelation effected? Not a court in Europe, not a Church in Christendom, not a philosophic Academy, not a scientific body, has acknowledged its claims or recognized its existence. Can the Eternal God make a revelation of his Will and his Word to his creatures, and the event not stir a ripple on the surface of human society? The fact is strange indeed, but it is not without precedent. The same God once visited this earth in person, with divine truth in his mouth and miraculous power in his hand, at the golden period of blended Greek and Roman civilization; and He was crucified as an obscure impostor! If they kill the Son himself, will they not stone his Prophets and insult his Messengers?

How are revelations made from heaven except by human mediums? Angels never speak to multitudes, but to individuals. God prepares certain pivotal or representative men for his work. Whether it be Noah or Abraham or Moses or John or Paul or another, every Dispensation has its beginning through a human medium; and this medium is almost invariably discredited by his brethren and persecuted by the world. Was it indeed ever otherwise? How strangely forgetful of history are those who imagine that a modern Prometheus, bringing new fire and light from heaven to men, could be received by them in any spirit but that of scoffing incredulity!

The Lord has in these latter times prepared a man, through whom he has revealed the spiritual sense of the Scriptures and the laws and phenomena of the Spiritual Life: the richest boon yet conferred on the human race. He was organized and trained from his birth for his wonderful mission. He co-existed consciously for many years, as we all do unconsciously, in both the spiritual and natural worlds. He met and conversed with angels and spirits as with men, and he recorded in one world what he saw and heard in the other. He is the John the Baptist of a New Dispensation, preparing the way of our Lord at his Second Coming.

Then arises the old doubt and incredulity, the sense of impossibility that one who lives under the same physical conditions with ourselves can enjoy any spiritual insight not common to us all. Is not this the son of the carpenter, and are not his brothers and sisters still with us? On this old ground every new truth is for a while rejected. But it matters not. The laws of Providence are the geometry of heaven. Nothing fails in its right time and in the right place. When the Hour comes, the Man also appears.

But why should this individual be so favored above his fellows? Simply because it is necessary and proper. Homers, Platos, Cæsars, Dantes, Shakspeares, Newtons, are not accidents. Their coming is as fixed and certain as the movement of the tides or the planets. Prophets, Apostles, and Seers are created for the spiritual exigencies of the race. One must do the work for millions. Individual revelations to all men are at present impracticable. Now, as in the ancient days, only Moses and Aaron can go up into the mountain to receive communications from God. The people and the priests must not come near the mountain to touch it, nor to "break through unto the Lord to gaze," lest they perish.

Swedenborg thus avows his extraordinary claim:

"The arcana which are revealed in the following pages relate to heaven and hell, and to the life of man after death. The members of the church at this day know scarcely any thing about heaven and hell, or about their own life after death,—although these things are all described in the Word. Many, though born within the church, even deny their existence, saying in their hearts, Who hath returned from them and declared the fact?

"Lest, therefore, such a negative state, which prevails mostly with those who possess much worldly wisdom, should also infect and corrupt the simple in heart and faith, I have been permitted to enter the society of angels, and to converse with them as one man converses with another, and also to see the things which exist in heaven and in hell. I have enjoyed this privilege for a period of thirteen years; and I am now permitted to describe the heavens and the hells from the testimony of my own sight and hearing, in the hope that ignorance may be thus enlightened and incredulity dissipated."

Fourteen years pass away, during which Swedenborg wrote and published a great deal, maintaining an unquestioned reputation for learning, wisdom, and virtue.

Subsequent to this he again emphatically defines his position:

"I foresee that many who read the Memorable Relations in this work will believe them to be fictions of the imagination; but I protest in truth that they are not fictions, but were really heard and seen. Not seen and heard in any state of the mind in sleep, but in a state of complete wakefulness; for it has pleased the Lord to manifest himself to me, and to send me to teach those things which belong to his New Church, which is meant by the New Jerusalem in the Revelation. For this purpose He has opened the interiors of my mind or spirit; by which privilege it has been permitted me to be with angels in the spiritual world and with men in the natural world at the same time, and that now for twenty-seven years."

In the trying and honest hour of death the great Seer bore unquailing witness to the truth of his wonderful mission. A worthy Lutheran clergyman was called in to administer the holy communion to the dying man. He observed to him, "That as many persons thought he had endeavored only to make himself a name by his New Theological System, he would do well now to publish the truth to the world, and to recant either the whole or a part of what he had advanced, since he had now nothing to expect from the world, which he was so soon about to leave for ever."

"On hearing these words, Swedenborg raised himself half-upright in bed, and placing the hand that was not paralyzed upon his breast, said with great zeal and emphasis:

"As true as you see me before you, so true is every thing I have written. I could have said more had I been permitted. When you come into eternity, you will see all things as I have stated and described them; and we shall have much to say concerning them to each other."

This was the closing scene. He retained his splendid faculties to the last. How inapplicable is our shocking word, death, to such a departure! He who had lived with both angels and men, was simply removed from men to live with angels for ever.

Swedenborg's System of Religious Philosophy, based upon a revealed spiritual interpretation of the Word of God, must stand upon its own merits. It is seen, like the sun, by its own light, and not by the light of another. Still, it is pleasant to those who receive it as the doctrinal basis of a New Dispensation of Divine Truth, to think that the medium or herald by whom it came, was one so worthy of his transcendent office; a man of such varied culture; such multiform wisdom; such practical and industrious utilities; of such abounding Christian virtues, and of such a tender and reverential spirit.

There are no traces of imposture or fanaticism or insanity in the life or the writings of this man. All the elements of credibility meet in his claims with the most extraordinary power. Not the least of these is the fact, that he teaches, as no man ever

4

taught before, the Supreme Divinity of Jesus Christ and the plenary inspiration of the Holy Scriptures. Whoever builds upon this sure foundation is not likely to build in vain.

This little volume is not designed to explain or to advocate the doctrines of Swedenborg. Our task is a far humbler one. We intend to take all his statements for granted, and to repeat what he has said about the heavenly country, so far as it may enable the reader to follow our lost ones into the spiritual realm. A small, small part indeed of the treasures of New Church truth do we here present. We are merely spies bringing specimen grapes from a land flowing with milk and honey.

"He that hath ears to hear, let him hear."

In one of those beautiful symbolic visions by which Swedenborg was taught interior truths, he beheld a splendid temple constructed of precious stones and with doors of solid pearl. Over the front was an inscription, "Nunc licet"—"It is now permitted."

He was told by his attendant angel, that thereby was signified the spiritual light and liberty of the New Church, which is to be the life and soul of a New Era. The human mind is henceforth permitted to criticise every theological dogma, and to demand a reason for every article of its faith. The reign of mystery is over. The spiritual despotisms of the Past are abolished. Science and Reason govern henceforth for ever under authority of a New Dispensation. The expanding mind of the race demands an explanation of the Word of God, an unfolding of the life to come, a reconciliation between Nature and Revelation. They have been granted. The Light has come. The glory of the Lord has shone round about us, and a little band of shepherds have seen the great Light, and have heard the heavenly host singing,

"Glory to God in the highest, and on earth peace, good-will toward men."

The source of this Light is the Lord Jesus Christ.

"I am come a Light into the world, that whosoever believeth on me shall not abide in darkness."

"And the city had no need of the sun, neither of the moon to shine in it; for the glory of God did lighten it."

It shines to us through the Holy Word as a medium:

"Open thou mine eyes, that I may behold wondrous things out of thy law."

And through angelic ministrations:

"Hereafter ye shall see heaven open."

This Light shines to us amidst all the surrounding darkness of false creeds and of skepticisms:

"And there was a thick darkness in all the land of Egypt; but all the children of Israel had light in their dwellings."

This Light is for the Lord's Last and Everlasting Church:

"The light of the moon shall be as the light of the sun, and the light of the sun shall be sevenfold."

"Thy sun shall no more go down: neither shall thy moon withdraw itself: for the Lord shall be thine everlasting Light."

This Light is Spiritual Truth. It must be revealed to man, for he can never discover it. It does not come from without, but from above and from within.

The Second Coming of the Lord is a manifestation of Spiritual Truth,—the new Light for a New Era.

CHAPTER II.

HOW ARE THEY RAISED?

THE Angel of Death comes and goes; intervening between God and us. His coming casts such a deep shadow; his going leaves such a strange light! The world is never the same to us before and after a great bereavement.

After the first wild exclamations of grief, how calm every one becomes! The vast burdens of anxious hope and fear and sympathy are removed. The nightmare of death is ended. The sufferings and agonies are all over. "After life's fitful fever, she sleeps well." We experience a stupefaction of mind which we mistake for serenity, whilst a larger, heavier burden is preparing for our hearts; the burden we only lay down with our own wearied bodies at the grave—the aching sense of separation.

Oh the unreality of what seems to us most real! the truth, the substantialty of spiritual things, which seem to us so shadowy!

With deep sighs the watchers now leave the bed-side. Their task is done: they need watch no more. The little figure lying there will never raise its head for a sip of water, nor open its eyes again to see if the dear familiar faces are around it. Take away the food and medicines; vain, useless, powerless things!—so lately the elixirs of hope and life. Prepare the drapery of the tomb. The women move about softly with whispered words or mere gestures, rendering the last offices of human kindness to the precious little body; embalming it with kisses, bathing it with tears.

Now it is ready, and all is quiet again. There it lies, cold and white, the deserted palace of the Soul! In the sweet, calm halo that surrounds it, sit the pensive watchers, scarcely ever exchanging a word. The night wears slowly away. The clock strikes the small hours one after another, breaking rudely with its mechanical voices upon the ethereal silence of sorrow.

At last the sad Dawn, pinning her gray mantle with a star, looks softly in at the shutters, starts back in gentle surprise, and lays her finger on her lips.

* * * * * *

Little Lucy was laid out in the parlor in the morning. The windows were thrown open, and the fresh air came in sweetly. Near her head stood a little table with the Holy Bible and a vase of fresh flowers upon it; both voices from heaven, speaking with unequal eloquence their consolations to the heart.

Sympathizing friends had sent in many offerings of flowers. What a precious token of kindly feeling is conveyed to a wounded heart by a mere present of flowers! Richer than words, almost equal to tears, are those beautiful hieroglyphics of the affections! The whole room was filled with their delicious perfume. They seemed striving to overshadow the cold fact of death by a spiritual presence, as if the emotions and thoughts of the departed child had passed into their beautiful and smiling forms.

The little body was almost buried in flowers. A splendid wreath of them crowned that golden head, "sunning over with curls." A rare bouquet had been placed in her tiny hands. She loved flowers instinctively, as angels and good men love poetry and music. Had she seen all that floral wealth and beauty showered on some little dead girl of her own sweet floral age, how she would have wept!

Her father, heart-worn with many watchings and

sorrows, came softly in and knelt by her side. He kissed her cold brow and her white cheek. A strange light shone from the little pale face; but, alas! it was only the daylight reflected from her beautiful, ethereal features. The soul's light had gone—was shining in another world, leaving darkness for him in this. He wept silently.

He sat thinking over the incidents of his little girl's short, sweet, beautiful life. The kaleidoscope of memory turned and turned, and many charming pictures rose up before him. He saw her baby face, round and rosy, nestling sweetly against her mother's breast. Then her first tottering expeditions from chair to chair, watched and applauded by all the family. She was now romping over the floor with shaggy little Fido; now rocking her doll, half as big as herself, with sober mother-face and earnest caressings. Suddenly she kissed her hand from the carriage, driving by, sweetly dressed and curled for the afternoon airing. Now he watches her serious brow poring over the pictures of the primer; then he hears her first, wandering, delicate touches at the piano, or the heavenly sweetness of her voice saying the Lord's Prayer. He gazes long at her fairy figure sporting on the green grass under the old whispering trees, gleaming to and fro like a sunbeam in their great shadows. These and many other sacred pictures of child-life passed slowly before him, touching and melting his innermost heart like the softest wails of cathedral music, stirring the divine despairs of the soul; and he wept bitterly.

He then went step by step, with fearful, torturing minuteness of detail, over all the incidents of her last terrible illness. Has grief its fascinations also, that we cannot help touching and teasing and tearing open the wounds of our own bleeding hearts? He retraced every thing that occurred, from day to day, from night to night; the fever, the thirst, the pain, the delirium; the whole onward and downward course of the hated disease; the mistakes, the failures, the omissions; the fears, the hopes, the supplications, the despairs; the last sad struggle and the frantic farewells. What a cup of agony! often emptied, always refilled. Will the joys of heaven through golden eternities efface these awful memories from the soul?

Then came the realization of the fact that the object of all this idolatry was gone for ever from the natural world. Gone for ever; invisible, inaccessible, seeming to have been annihilated! It is fearful to lose a child in the streets of a great city, where pursuit is possible, and where a thousand eager feet join you in the search. But your child steps out of your sight into the wilderness of the spiritual world, and none can pursue it but your own aching, weary, bleeding heart—alone and in vain, through long, bitter years, seemingly unaided by God or angels or men.

Is my child really still alive in the face of all this apparent death? Has she the same spiritual vitality she had a few days ago? or is she asleep, every faculty being dormant until a resurrection in some far future? These and kindred questions pressed for solution on his heart.

Suddenly his eye fell upon the family Bible, which little Lucy had often put upon his knees, begging him to read of little Moses floating among the rushes, or of little Samuel startled in the night by the voice of the Lord. She loved the charming narratives of the Scripture, and her bright blue eyes would often turn reverently upwards at the mention of sacred things.

She used to gaze curiously upon the entry made in that Bible of her birthday, as if innocently wondering how such a trifle as her birthday could be recorded in the same volume with so many holy and beautiful things. Alas! the death-page, then so white, had a line waiting for her little name also.

The Word of God exists in heaven as well as upon earth—a fact quite unknown to the present Christian church. Here it is veiled in simple and sometimes uncomely forms: but there it is the very mind and thought of God, the source of all truth.

Of that Bible in heaven—the soul, to which our earthly Bible is the homely body—Swedenborg beautifully says:

"There are many wonderful phenomena resulting from the Word in the spiritual world. The Word itself, kept in the most sacred recesses of the temples in that world, shines in the sight of the angels like a great star, and sometimes like a sun. It sometimes also seems to be encompassed by beautiful rainbows. This phenomenon is exhibited so soon as ever the sacred repository of the Word is opened."

No outward rainbows encircled that old family Bible to the bereaved father's eye, but a great light came from it upon his soul, when he opened its pages on that eventful morning.

Kneeling by the dead body of his beloved daughter, he took the sacred Volume in his hands, and prayed the Lord, with a deep, agonizing, living faith, to give him one sentence, one word of comfort, of strength, from his written Word; some light, some knowledge of his darling's whereabouts or welfare; some strong and sure breathing of peace upon him from that happy sphere where all is peace.

He opened the Book at random, and by that kind of chance which is providence, he put his finger on the forty-first verse of the fifth chapter of Mark:

"And he took the damsel by the hand, and said unto her, Talitha cumi; which is, being interpreted, Damsel (I say unto thee), arise!"

With the sacred verse there came shining down into his heart a clear, sweet perception of the fact that at that very moment the Lord Jesus Christ, who alone is the Resurrection and the Life, was raising up out of her cold and lifeless form that beautiful, spiritual body in which little Lucy will exist as an angel for ever.

He plucked some white and green leaves from the flowers which lay in the dead child's hand, and placed them on that verse of the sacred Volume. Years have passed away, and they are there still, pale and withered; sacred little mementoes of the consolation which came like a voice from heaven in his hour of need. When he is haunted by sorrowful memories and falls into states of desolation and despair, he opens that Holy Book and kisses those faded leaves; and his spirit is sometimes elevated into that mount which the three disciples ascended spiritually with their Lord, and there, by the permission of the same great Redeemer, who makes every child of his an image of himself, he sees the body of his little daughter transfigured in glory.

If the material body rises no more, once inquired a thoughtless mother, why should we lavish such attention and care upon the sepulchre? The answer is simple. How tenderly we treasure the garments, the play-things, the books, the portraits of our lost children! How much more tenderly should we care for that little handful of sacred dust in which their dear spirits once lived and moved and communed with us!

In a sweet, silent spot of a southern graveyard, where there is verdure nearly all the year round, and the shadow of great trees, and the song of birds, three little mounds are seen. They are colored all over with petunias and heart's-ease. Their marble head-pieces shine softly in the gloom. The name of Lucy, sweet as a little flower, is engraved on one of them. On her baby-brother's monument appear the true, true words:

"HE IS NOT HERE: HE IS RISEN."

Yes! our graves have no human tenants. No man, woman, or child, since the beginning of the world was ever really buried. The dust and ashes which they temporarily inhabited have been properly consigned to the tomb; but the soul, the man, the living being, has past out of it for ever.

Away with the degrading falsehood that human beings are sleeping in the grave! The phraseology is revolting and hateful. The old Greek poet, without the light of revelation, knew better:

"Proté, thou art not dead; but hast removed to a better place, and dwellest in the Islands of the Blest, among abundant banquets, where thou art delighted; tripping along the Elysian plains among soft flowers, free from every ill."

"How shall we bury you?" said Crito to Socrates, before he drank the poison. "Just as you please," replied the Philosopher, "if you can ever catch me."

Two very different scenes are enacted around every dead body on the two sides of the great curtain which separates the natural from the spiritual world.

On one side we have the dark trappings of woe; the solemn hearse, the funeral crape, the sad procession, the wails of grief, the priestly promise of some far-off resurrection, the dreadful "earth to earth, ashes to ashes, dust to dust."

Nothing of this appears on the other side; nothing of this is possible. Angels and good spirits occupy an altogether different stand-point. To their perceptions our death is a birth, our departure an arrival, our burial a resurrection. The grave for them has no existence; life no break in its continuous current. They look on us merely as travelers coming up from a lower sphere, and they welcome us gladly to their glorious habitations.

Not only the fact that we have a spiritual body conjoined to our natural body during life, and separated from it at death, has been revealed to man, but also the very process by which the separation or resurrection takes place.

Swedenborg makes the following wonderful and solemn affirmation:

"In what manner resuscitation is effected has not only been related to me, but has also been shown to me by actual experience. I was myself made the subject of that experience, in order that I might fully know how the great change is accomplished.

"I was brought into a state of insensibility as

to the bodily senses, and thus nearly into the state of dying persons. The interior life, however, remained entire, together with the faculty of thought, that I might observe and retain in my memory the particulars of the process I was about to undergo, which was exactly such as is experienced by those who are being resuscitated from the dead."

Death is no longer a leap in the dark to those who accept the Lord's new revelations of the life to come. We need not gaze on the dead faces of our friends in blank wonder and despair. We can follow them in imagination into the spiritual world almost as surely as we could follow them into England or Italy. By the genial light of a New Dispensation let us strip death of its sting and the grave of its victory. Let us see what happened to our precious little ones when their eyelids dropped for ever upon the scenes of this lower world.

When the heart ceases to beat and the lungs to breathe, it is a sign that the spiritual body can no longer abide with its living currents of affection and thought in its earthly tenement. It can no more see through the windows of the material eye, or hear the music of this world through that cunning instrument, the natural ear. It lies in a deep, dreamless sleep, waiting for some heavenly touch to awaken it to its interior and real life. This sleep is of short duration.

Now a beautiful and wonderful thing occurs. Two or more glorious angels from the Lord's celestial kingdom, the kingdom in which Love is the breath of life, descend from their happy homes on the sweetest errand of mercy. The life of the angels is the love of uses. Selfishness and death are with them synonymous. Their offices, employments, and duties, all for the good of others, are of infinite variety. Many of them are engaged in secret and constant services to the human race. There are angels of birth and death; angels who comfort in sickness and sorrow; angels who instruct and enlighten; angels who defend from evil spirits and devils; angels who lead the sweet thoughts of innocent children; angels who inspire conjugial love; and a thousand other genera and species of heavenly ministers.

Those who approach are angels of the resurrection.

They sit near the head and feet of the little spirit, whose spiritual body, no longer animating its natural form, now first becomes visible in the light of the spiritual world. They do not speak, but gaze into its face, ready to communicate their own peace and love, by processes altogether spiritual, to the resuscitating soul as soon as it becomes conscious. They do not see the natural body, the little corpse, any more than we, who are weeping over the latter, can see the purer spiritual body at which they are gazing. Each side, so real in its own sphere, is invisible, imperceptible to the other.

A delightful odor of flowers and aromatic spices surrounds the spiritual body on the approach of those radiant inhabitants of heaven. Their holy sphere keeps at a distance all evil spirits who might attempt to pry into or to interfere with the wonderful process about to be effected. These angels take possession of what Swedenborg calls the region of the heart. Spiritually, this means the whole emotional nature of the man, which they regulate and control for the time, subduing every thing to a sacred calm. They await in silence and joy the great event, the extraction of a spiritual body from its material envelope, its prison or grave, and its birth into the spiritual world.

The resurrection is effected by the Lord alone. That little spiritual body lying there in its dreamless sleep, could never move or see or hear or feel again, unless the Lord withdrew it from its entanglement in the meshes of its physical form. The angels might call and pray and labor in vain. They could not wake it. The Lord alone is the Resurrection and the Life.

The resurrection is effected by a powerful attraction. It was felt by Swedenborg as a steady and strong drawing or pulling, a veritable extraction, as sensibly as if he were drawing his arm out of a sleeve. The withdrawal of the winged butterfly out of its first groveling form, which it never more resumes, was regarded by ancient wisdom as typical of the ascension into heaven of the spiritual body or soul after renouncing its material envelope.

But this attraction by the Lord?

How little we realize in our poor, dark, sensual earth-state, that there is really no life in the universe but the Lord's! Our heat is only the Lord's love let down from heaven into our vibrating ethers. Our light is nothing but the Lord's wisdom or spiritual light, moving about amongst our organic atoms, and revealing to us somewhat of the mysteries and beauties of his creation. All our physical forces, so called, are simply spiritual forces, playing and flowing and working through natural media. Repulsion and attraction, those secret mother-springs of all physical, chemical, and physiological phenomena, come first of all from the Lord, and are modes or laws of His own divine life.

His outbreathing, or desire to create all things by emanations from Himself (repulsion), is the centrifugal force of the spiritual spheres. His indrawing, or desire to unite and assimilate all things created to Himself (attraction), is the centripetal force of the same realms. When the bonds, weights, or clogs which confined the soul to the material sphere are broken or dissolved at death, it ascends upwards and inwards in obedience to spiritual attraction. If our earth should suddenly fall into nothingness under our feet, our bodies would be drawn into the sun, unless attracted and caught in the sphere of some nearer planet. So our spiritual forms, ceasing to animate their natural bodies, are drawn out of them by divine attraction, and are caught in the magnetic love-sphere of sympathetic spiritual societies.

Behold the secret of the resurrection! which necessarily takes place immediately after the death of the material body.

The expectant angels perceive by the movements of the face that the spirit is beginning to emerge into consciousness again. With eager pleasure they impart to it their own sphere of unutterable serenity and peace; for in the other life affections and thoughts radiate and are reflected or absorbed just as the rays of light are in this. The painful or stormy elements of human passion are all quiescent, and every soul awakes into the inner life, as if breathing an enchanted atmosphere and listening to heavenly music. These celestial angels detain the mind of the new comer as long as possible in this holy and happy frame; and if he sinks into a sphere of baser feeling and lower thought, it is by his own volition.

None but celestial angels, those who are highest and purest and nearest to the Lord, could so officiate in this solemn and beautiful event, as to ward off every evil influence and to surround the helpless, newly-revived spirit with a protective atmosphere of peace and love.

These tender cares are shown to every human being who departs from this world, no matter where, or when, or how the great exit is made. Whether they were good or evil, great or humble, bond or free; whether they died by battle or murder or shipwreck, at home or abroad, happily or miserably; whether they passed away with prayers or curses on their lips, with love or hatred in their hearts; they all sink into the same deep, sweet sleep, and are guarded and welcomed by celestial angels. From that point they all diverge, and each seeks the good or evil societies congenial to his interior nature; but all are born or ushered into the world of spirits in the same manner and under the same sweet influences.

Our Lord himself, who subjected His divine nature to the limitations of time and space, who suffered in a human form, and was tempted in all things as we are, who died and was buried, received in His own resurrection the same kind services from the celestial angels, according to the universal law. For Mary, stooping down to look into the sepulchre, saw "two angels in white sitting, one at the head and the other at the feet, where the body of Jesus had lain."

The task of the celestial angels is now done. These glorious beings are too pure and holy for the new-comer from our sinful world to have any intimate communion with them at first. As the interior nature of the novitiate spirit unfolds itself, the dissimilar spheres repel, and the celestial angels seem to retire to their own abodes, to start again on their labor of love. The risen spirit passes under the tutelage of the spiritual angels, who now appear and take charge of him with every demonstration of affectionate interest.

Hitherto after waking, the resuscitated soul had only been able to feel and think, but not to see. Why this brief blindness? Because as a general rule (to which, indeed, there are exceptions), we can see only those in the spiritual world whose state of life is near akin to our own. Only the pure in heart can see God. The sphere of the celestial angels is darkness to those who are not celestial. We may safely infer that infants and small children, in whose minds no external or scientific sphere of thought has yet been formed, and in whom the celestial degree or plane of life is still open, do not experience this transitory deprivation of sight.

The spiritual angels live in palaces of precious stones resplendent with all beautiful colors. They flow into and govern the thoughts, as the celestial angels do the affections. They operate on the understanding as the celestials do on the will. They are literally angels of light. It is their business and their delight to instruct. The love of truth is the supreme passion of their souls.

They restore the just-liberated spiritual body to sight. They seem to roll off a kind of membrane from the eye, and to draw something very gently off from the face. This, however, is merely an appearance, whereby is represented the change from natural to spiritual thought. Spiritual light, which is seven-fold brighter than the light of our noonday sun, now bursts upon the vision of the delighted spirit. What a world of beauty and wonder! With what amazement is he filled! What an escape from the dark caverns and pitfalls and shadows of our lower realm, into

> "An ampler ether, a diviner air,
> And fields invested with purpureal gleams!"

The angels now tell the spirit that he is an inhabitant of the spiritual world, and answer his thousand eager inquiries about every thing around him. They summon his friends and relatives who have preceded him across the river of death, and there are such greetings as are never witnessed in this world, and can never be described in human language. He is overwhelmed with kindnesses, hospitalities, and civilities, until he passes gradually, and almost unconsciously to himself, into that terrible process of judgment which strips him of all false appearances and deceptive values, exposes his naked heart to his own view and that of others, and assigns him to the place he had prepared for himself by his life and conduct in the world.

Whatever may be the final issue, we may rest assured that the first state of all men after death is a state of wonder and delight. At the time when we are saddest, our deceased friends are most joyful. When we see only death, they see nothing but life. When we are recounting our loss, they are revolving their gain. When our darkness is deepest, their light is brightest. When our despair is wildest, their hope is unbounded.

Spirits from Christian countries are especially bewildered at finding themselves in possession of what seems to them the same body they had in the world. They feel, hear, see, just as they did before. They have the same shape, size, color, hair, hands, feet; indeed, all the organs of the human body. Every thing about them seems as solid and real as it ever was here. It is hard to convince them that they are dead and in another world, because the change is so totally unlike what they expected. The most learned prelates and philosophers are more amazed than the unthinking multitude unaccustomed to metaphysical subtleties.

Why is this?

Because in the Christian churches at the present day there is no knowledge of the real nature of spirit and the spiritual world. They expect no revelation on the subject, and indeed for the most part desire none. They are content to take the Bible as their moral guide, to interpret it literally as best they can, and to defer all acquaintance with the other life until they actually enter upon that life. They have no conception of the spirit or soul as an organized human form composed of spiritual substance; nor of heaven as a real, substantial spiritual world. By abstracting goodness, wisdom, and virtue from their forms or subjects, they imagine that spirits can love and know, feel and think, without any genuine embodiment whatever.

They are of course astonished at death to find that man has a spiritual body organized for eternal life in a spiritual world, to which a natural body was attached during the first or material stage of his existence. With a spiritual body dwelling in a suitable and eternal spiritual world, there is of course no use of the cast-off natural body any more; no general resurrection from the material grave; no destruction of the physical universe; no second coming of the Lord into nature, as misinterpretations of the letter of the Word have taught the Christian church to expect.

Is not the world spiritually starving for a new, rational, thorough, and practical revelation of the life to come, when we find such an inscription as this on a tombstone in a Christian city, quoted from the hymns of a Christian poet?—

> "There are no acts of pardon passed
> In the cold grave to which we haste;
> But darkness, death, and long despair
> Dwell in eternal silence there."

How sweetly, swiftly does the pure heart of childhood get at the clear truth, when it realizes no essential difference between the forms, feelings, and life of the other world and of this!

"Good-bye, dear papa!" said a lovely little boy, as his dying eyes turned from a golden sunset. "Good-bye, dear papa! I am going to mother. We will all meet in the morning."

Yes, dear friends! it is true. We will all meet in the Morning.

CHAPTER III.

WHAT BODIES HAVE THEY?

O BEREAVED mother! thinking of the beautiful little form you have just laid in the grave, and weeping over the little garments it wore, as one by one you fold them away—things henceforth of memory and not of use—suppose your natural senses could be laid asleep, as in the magnetic trance, and your spiritual eyes opened into heaven, into the very mansion and chamber where your child is, what would you expect to see?

Some shadowy, vapory space, filled with aerial music and songs of praise? peopled by vague abstractions of goodness and virtue, possibly the souls of men? and your little one, a disembodied spirit, almost or quite intangible, floating or flying hither and thither, waiting for its reunion with a fleshly body?

The Old Dispensations can give us little better light than this; broken moonlight flickering on the water. Turn away from these glimmerings, and behold the real state of things in the sweet sunshine of spiritual truth.

You would see a chamber furnished with articles of indescribable beauty, in comparison with which the wonders of imperial palaces are trifles. You would see an angel-woman, in whose radiant and heavenly presence you could scarcely lift up your eyes, and the tones of whose voice would melt you into tears. In her arms you would see the very child you thought you had buried in the dust. Nothing would be lost, nothing absent. Every golden curl would be found in its place; every dimple on its exquisitely-moulded limbs; the old smiles on its ethereal lips; the same joyous spring in its motions; the same dreamy heaven of love and peace in its eyes.

You would at first suppose it was a beautiful dream or a vision. When you became convinced that the scene was real, and not imaginary, you would not understand how your child could be living and dead at the same time. You would not remember its duplicate body, the natural form laid in the grave and resolving into dust. You would think your child had been miraculously spirited away into that wonderful place. You would be frantic for its possession. When your spiritual eyes were closed again, the old gulf would yawn between you; and all would be dark for a moment. Then you would find yourself in your own chamber, weeping over the fragments of your broken hope; and you would call your spiritual experience a dream!

"If they hear not Moses and the Prophets, neither will they be persuaded though one rose from the dead."

We can never follow our little ones satisfactorily into the other life, until we grasp the beautiful idea, that the spiritual body is a human form organized of spiritual substance, and inhabiting a spiritual universe, which may interpenetrate the physical universe without having any connection with it perceptible to our natural senses.

Before considering the wonderful and beautiful changes which the spiritual body undergoes after death, we must fix clearly in our minds the fact that the soul of man has two garments, an inner and an outer one. The latter, or the natural body, may be parted and destroyed. The former, or spiritual body, in which all life, thought, feeling really abide, like the inner raiment of our Lord, is without seam and indestructible. The co-existence of these two bodies during our earth-life and their separation at death, is the central truth about which as a golden pivot a rational Psychology must revolve.

"There *is* a natural body and there *is* a spiritual body," is the true formula of Christian faith; and not its strange perversion,—"there is a natural body which shall be miraculously changed into a spiritual one." "Thou sowest not that body that shall be," says Paul. The exterior body perishes, falling off like a glove from the hand, whilst the interior rises and lives for ever.

The co-existence of these bodies is the key to the relation between mind and matter; the spiritual and natural worlds. It throws a flood of light upon many passages of Scripture hitherto involved in mystery. It explains the true ground of the credibility of the Prophets and Seers—including Swedenborg—who profess to have received instruction from the spiritual side of the universe, by hearing or open vision. "In my spirit in the midst of my body," is the singular form of expression by which Daniel refers to his troubled visions.

To be living in the natural world, and to have the spiritual eyes and ears so opened into heaven as to see and converse with angels face to face!

How the gross and sensual spirit of this age shrinks with incredulity from the recognition of such a claim! The idea of a man's reporting the state of things in heaven, say they, as a traveler would report the condition of India! Why not? As if heaven were not nearer than India! As if heaven were not within us, and the road to it through our own souls! As if the good and beautiful things of earth would continue for a moment unless the breath of heaven kept them persistent in form and shining in use! As if our own affections and thoughts were not already, according to their character, in heaven or hell, and we ourselves unconsciously members of some spiritual society in one world or the other! As if—oh, shameful naturalism!—heaven were some distant locality only to be reached by actual transference through natural space!

Our own spiritual bodies are the hidden gates which lead into and out of the spiritual kingdom. We have eyes within our eyes which can see the glorious landscapes of Heaven. We have ears within our ears which can hear the ineffable hallelujahs of the Redeemed. We are so constituted also, that the angels of those inner realms may, under circumstances of rare occurrence, look through our eyes as through windows, and see the poor baubles of our earthly architecture, and hear through our ears the miserable wails of human suffering.

The existence of this wonderful duality of universes; of an invisible and a visible world blended together by corresponding forms; of a spiritual body and a natural body co-existing, is recognized by the poet in his most exalted states, and runs in slender threads of beauty and truth here and there through the songs of all nations.

Shelley gives this idea in one of its phases very charming expression, when the Spirit of the Earth says to Prometheus:

> "——— Ere Babylon was dust,
> The Magus Zoroaster, my dead child,
> Met his own image walking in the garden.
> That apparition, sole of men, he saw;
> For know, there are two worlds of life and death:
> One, that which thou beholdest; the other
> Is far beyond the grave, where do inhabit
> The shadows of all forms that think and live.
> * * * * * * *
> Terrible, strange, sublime, and beauteous shapes!
> There thou art, and dost hang, a writhing shade,
> 'Mid whirlwind-peopled mountains: all the gods
> Are there; and all the powers of nameless worlds,
> Vast sceptred phantoms: heroes, men and beasts."

Descending from the region of fancy to that of

fact, between which the truth lies, always touching on both, we can verify the existence of another body within our physical bodies by asking any mutilated soldier, whether he does not feel the wholeness, the unity of his body and limbs as before. He will tell us that he feels his limb exactly as if it were not amputated. Our scientific men try to explain this by saying it is a physiological law, that sensations really occurring in the nervous centres are referred to the peripheries or circumference. But here the periphery or circumference has no physical existence, because it has been amputated. It is to the real but invisible circumference, the arm or leg of the spiritual body, that the sensation is referred.

A higher Physiology, which is among the better things coming, will discover that all life, sensation, thought, and volition occur in the spiritual body, and are manifested outwardly through the natural body as a medium or machine, which has no life in itself, but derives its life, moment by moment, from the spiritual form within it.

These spiritual bodies of ours, living in our material forms, are seldom visible to the spirits who are in nearest attendance upon us, because we think and feel so differently from them, so entirely in time and space; we are so drawn, so abstracted from spiritual things by the love, care, and necessity of earthly things, that they cannot see us. Similarity of thought and affection makes proximity and presence in the other life. Still we do sometimes become obscurely visible to our spirit friends in certain states of great mental quiescence or abstraction. They also have *their* ghosts or apparitions. Some friend in heaven suddenly sees his friend living on earth standing or walking apart, silent and not looking toward him. He gazes a while, as we would at a spirit, half in fear, half in wonder. He calls out to him, and the figure vanishes. The earthly friend starts at the same moment from his reverie, and wonders whether or not he heard the voice of some one calling him.

The opening of the spiritual senses, the sight, hearing, touch, &c., of the spiritual body, may be partial or complete. The ear alone may be opened, and nothing seen. The little child Samuel hears the Lord calling him, and receives a message for Eli; but sees nothing. Sometimes the eye alone is opened, but nothing heard. The men who were with Paul when he was struck to the earth saw the great light, but did not hear the voice of Jesus speaking to his persecutor.

Sometimes the eye is only opened so far as to see a light, but not the person or figure of the spiritual speaker. Moses saw a fire in the bush and heard the angelic voice, but did not see the angel. Sometimes there is no light, but the figure or person of a spirit or angel appears. In this case the spirit seems to be in the natural world with us; but he is not, and cannot see or feel any thing of our surroundings except through our own minds.

A still further degree of insight (sight from within) is when the appearing spirit or angel can exhibit various spiritual objects to the eye for purposes of instruction. Ezekiel and other Prophets, and St. John in the Isle of Patmos, enjoyed this intercourse to a wonderful degree. But the highest state of spiritual communication is when all the senses of the spiritual body are opened at once into the spiritual sphere, and not only spirits or angels are seen, but also the scenery, houses, cities, &c., of the heavenly world. This was the case with Swedenborg for more than a quarter of a century.

Many curious mental phenomena which are mysteries to the present incapable psychology, and are therefore shelved as traditions, superstitions, or impostures, may be explained as partial openings of our interior senses. Many wonderful things told of apparitions, trances, dreams, witchcraft, magic, mesmerism, somnambulism, &c., find here their solution. It frequently happens also that the dying have partial intromission into the spiritual spheres, and see their departed friends and hear the music of heaven; not with their natural eyes and ears, as the wondering bystanders ignorantly suppose, but with the opening senses of the spiritual body.

This grand revelation through Swedenborg of the nature and functions of the spiritual body, is a key to some of the strangest and most difficult portions of the Bible. Many things which appear miraculous, or as violating the fixed laws of nature, can be shown to be manifestations of spiritual truths, occurring actually and solely in the spiritual sphere, but ignorantly referred to our external and natural plane of life and thought.

To illustrate: Moses, a meek and sorrowful exile, is quietly feeding his flock in a solitary place upon Mount Horeb, "the mountain of God;" brooding, perchance, over the cruel bondage of his brethren in Egypt. Suddenly a wonderful thing appears to him, a bright flame of fire bursting out of the midst of a bush. Wholly unconscious that the real cause of this phenomenon is a change occurring in his own spirit, he is filled with amazement. The fire continues to burn brightly, but "the bush is not consumed," for the simple reason that there is no natural fire in it. Moses, however, thinks it is a natural fire; and he approaches, as he says, "to see this great sight, why the bush is not burned." Suddenly a voice calls to him out of the bush, and after commanding him to take off his shoes from his feet, proceeds to charge him with a great and solemn mission.

Moses describes the scene precisely as it appeared to his own senses. The real state of the case was this: The Lord sent an angel filled with his Spirit, so as to speak in his name. He approaches Moses from his spiritual side,—for no angel or spirit can resume any physical embodiment, or be seen by the natural eye of man. The spiritual sight of Moses is first partially opened, and he sees the burning bush. The divine light flowing down into the external or scientific sphere of his own mind, is represented symbolically to him as a fire burning in a bush which is not consumed. When his spiritual hearing is opened, he holds the conversation with the angel of the Lord, detailed in Exodus. If some wanderer in the desert had approached the spot, he would have seen no fire and have heard no voice. If his sight alone had been opened, like the attendants of Paul, he would have seen the light, but would not have heard the words.

After our Lord's resurrection, it is stated that sundry persons came out of their graves and appeared to many. Was this a genuine flesh-and-blood resurrection before the appointed time? Did these people go back into their graves, and resume the long sleep to which the Old Theology consigns them? The explanation is this: After the crucifixion, the spiritual sight of a great many of the disciples was partially opened. They saw the angels about the sepulchre, and indeed the Lord himself, with their spiritual eyes. They saw his ascension to heaven in the same manner; for He certainly never rose into the physical atmosphere! They saw certain old saints with the same eyes; and knowing they had been dead and buried (as the natural man will have it) for a long time, they inferred that they must have risen from their graves. Having no correct idea of the spiritual body or the spiritual world, and being wholly unconscious of the changes occurring in their own spirits, they regarded as miracles certain events, which were simply the operation of spiritual laws with which they were unacquainted.

In our blind faith and reverence for Moses and

Ezekiel, John and Paul, we suppose they understood the whole deep philosophy and wonderful mechanism of the Revelation they were instrumental in making. This is a great error. The Prophets and Apostles were generally simple-minded, uncultivated men, who interpreted in a sensuous manner, according to the strict literal appearance, things which were beyond their interior comprehension. It was their mission to give the Word of God its external or sensuous basis; and there is no special reason why, or probability that they understood it themselves in any other manner.

We must get rid of prophet-worship and apostle-worship, as well as of hero-worship and saint-worship. Those worthies were the passive mediums, not the authors of Revelation. Our faith, our reverence, our love, must be felt not for their persons or characters any further than they naturally deserve, but for the spiritual truths they have communicated,—frequently not knowing their real value,—and for the Lord, from whom those truths descended, flowing from sphere to sphere, from heaven to heaven, from angels and spirits to man on earth in his lowest and simplest degree of life.

The doctrine of the spiritual body must be made

clear to our minds, before the glorious light of Swedenborg's revelations can fall upon the vital questions of life which so vex our inmost hearts. His own mission and seership become possible and credible to us only when we understand the mechanism as it were of his spiritual insight. The credibility of his teachings must rest on their inherent truth; but a prior difficulty in every mind, is the question of the possibility of his supernatural communications. We have so long regarded the other life as "the bourne whence no traveler returns," and its phenomena as the incommunicable secrets of the grave, that we are accustomed to view with distrust any claim to spiritual experience.

We see the biblical narratives of open vision through the enchanting distances of time and space, and whatever interpretation we give them, we are unwilling to admit that any thing similar can happen in our own age and country. This is unphilosophical and unreasonable. The same organic mental constitution—the spiritual body connecting the soul with both heaven and hell—exists in all men; in Abraham, in Moses, in Paul, in Swedenborg, in ourselves. Every human being has a potentiality of seeing into heaven and hell without any change of place; without any violation of general laws, spiritual or natural; by merely having some dormant faculties of his being excited into action. Oh how ignorant we all are of the latent heat, the latent light, the latent electricities and magnetisms of the Human Soul!

There are two wonderful narratives, one in the Old, the other in the New Testament, which beautifully illustrate and are illustrated by this doctrine of the spiritual body. Their exposition is not only interesting in itself, making clear what was dark before, but it will unfold the very process by which Swedenborg's eyes were opened into the spiritual world.

Elijah and Elisha, the old Prophet and his disciple, walk along down to the river Jordan, conversing about the wonderful event impending, the instantaneous translation of Elijah to heaven. Fifty sons of the prophets come along also, to view afar off the wonderful scene. Elijah and Elisha cross the Jordan, the fifty witnesses remaining behind.

Elijah, aware of his approaching dissolution, says to Elisha,

"Ask what I shall do for thee, before I be taken away from thee."

Elisha replies:

"I pray thee, let a double portion of thy spirit be upon me."

The old Prophet, knowing well from long experience how spiritual vision was effected, responds:

"Thou hast asked a hard thing: nevertheless, if thou see me when I am taken from thee, it shall be so unto thee: but if not, it shall not be so."

This seems like a very strange answer. There they stand in the open light of day. Fifty witnesses are looking on beyond the little river. If chariots and horsemen were coming to take the physical body of Elijah into heaven, what was to hinder Elisha and the fifty witnesses watching across the river from seeing every thing that occurred?

Elijah knew that his translation could not be seen with the natural eye. He knew that unless Elisha's spiritual eyes were opened, he could not possibly see the spiritual conveyance which was coming for him. He knew that the Lord alone could open his spiritual eyes and make his ascent heavenward visible. That opening of the spiritual eyes would be a sign that Elisha would inherit the prophetical office. He would then be a Seer—one who sees things which others do not and cannot see.

The expected event takes place. Elisha sees the chariots and horsemen of Israel; he sees the spiritual (not the natural body) of Elijah ascend: he catches the falling mantle; he thinks—for so it appeared from his stand-point—that Elijah ascended bodily into heaven: for no man has any consciousness of the opening of his spiritual eyes. It seems to him that he sees objects as before with his natural eyes.

Not so, however, the fifty bystanders across the little river, whose spiritual eyes were not opened; but who were straining their natural eyes to see all that was to be seen. They saw no chariot, no horsemen, no ascending Elijah. They saw a whirlwind, and no doubt the material body of Elijah, abandoned by its spiritual form, carried aloft and away. So fully persuaded were they that the Spirit of the Lord had cast Elijah's body away off on some mountain or valley, that they entreated Elisha to permit them to go in search of it. Viewing the matter from a different stand-point, he at first refused. They insisted: he consented: and they searched three days in vain. Neither party saw the whole transaction. The evidence of both is necessary to make it intelligible.

Again: our Lord takes three favorite lisciples

with him up into a high mountain; and as He prays, an astounding change takes place in his personal appearance. His garments become "white and glistering," and "his face did shine as the sun."

Moses and Elias then become visible and talk with him about his approaching crucifixion. After a while the vision disappears, and the amazed disciples find themselves alone with Jesus in his usual form.

The disciples narrated the event just as it appeared to their senses. They believed, and the Apostolic Church believes to this day, that the natural body and clothing of our Lord underwent some miraculous transformation; and that Moses and Elias came down from heaven in some incomprehensible way, and appeared bodily to the natural eye on a mountain of Judea. The disciples did not know, nor do the majority of Christians today suspect, that the real change took place in the spiritual sight of the witnesses themselves. No one whose spiritual eyes were not open, would have seen or heard any thing which there and then happened. Had such a person, rambling about the mountain, stumbled on the party and watched them, unseen himself, he would have conscientiously pronounced the strange story of the disciples a gross fabrication or a wild hallucination of the senses.

Before they saw the wonders of the transfiguration, their external senses were laid asleep; for says the Evangelist: "They were heavy with sleep; and when they were awake, they saw his glory and the two men that stood with him." Again, it is recorded that as the scene passed away, "a cloud overshadowed them." This momentary darkness or sleep at the beginning and end of spiritual vision, is common. It is described by Swedenborg as occurring in his own case; and is caused, no doubt, by the transition, in the first place, from natural to spiritual sight, and in the second, back again from spiritual to natural vision.

The disciples saw the glorious Spiritual Body of our Lord, such as it appears now to the angels in heaven, when they get into those elevated states of feeling and thought representated by ascending a very high mountain. They saw the spiritual bodies of Moses and Elias, and they heard the conversation between them and Jesus with their spiritual ears. John saw and heard the wonders of the Apocalypse in the same manner. A bystander would not have shared the sights or the sounds with him, and would no doubt have pronounced him insane.

These and many other similar cases recorded in the Word—unintelligible mysteries when viewed from the literal stand-point—embody the very laws and phenomena of the life to come. They contain the germinal points of the only rational psychology; but a faithless generation, a degenerate church, an unbelieving world, class them with visions and compare them to dreams!

The apostle Paul's naïve version of his own case is strongly confirmatory of Swedenborg's statements, which throw back on it a reciprocal light, making it more intelligible.

"I will come to visions and revelations from the Lord. I knew a man in Christ above fourteen years ago (whether in the body, I cannot tell; or whether out of the body, I cannot tell: God knoweth); such an one caught up to the third heaven.

"And I knew such a man (whether in the body or out of the body, I cannot tell: God knoweth),

"How that he was caught up into paradise, and heard unspeakable words, which it is not lawful [or, more correctly translated, *is not possible*] for a man to utter."

Paul's external senses are made quiescent, and

he visits in the spiritual body, just as Swedenborg did, the angels of the third or highest heaven. He cannot understand his condition. He knows he is not dead, for he is still on the earth. He knows he has been to heaven, for he conversed with angels. He felt himself to be in the same body while in heaven; and still he could not imagine how that heavy, material form could have been caught up into paradise, where he heard and saw such wonderful things. His mind was not enlightened as to the nature or method of his elevation; and he never knew in this life whether he had been "in the body or out of the body."

Swedenborg states also that the wisdom or light of the angels in the third heaven is so great, that it is incommunicable to those from inferior spheres. When spirits are elevated thither by certain methods, they see and hear what Paul did, and understand it all while in mental rapport with the inhabitants; but so soon as they return to their own inferior places, it either escapes their memory entirely, or it is impossible for them to clothe the ideas in intelligible language. This was the case with Paul. He heard things when his spiritual ears were opened, which, in his ordinary natural state, he found it "impossible to utter."

The great Apostle's apparently fruitless visit to the celestial spheres was a precious legacy to the Church; embodying the sublime and almost forgotten truth, that it is possible for a man while living in this world to be caught up into paradise, to see and hear the wonders of heaven, and to continue a long while afterwards to discharge his duties upon earth. This first recorded visit, this mere peep into the highest heaven, was prophetic of the thorough and prolonged intercourse with the world of spirits vouchsafed seventeen hundred years after to another servant of the Lord Jesus Christ.

Swedenborg's spiritual eyes were opened in the year 1743, and so continued, with an intermission of but a few days, until his death in 1772, a period of twenty-nine years. His pure and peaceful life had been earnestly devoted to scientific and philosophical pursuits. He had never paid any special attention to theology; and this new and strange mission, for which he had been silently prepared by the Divine Providence, came upon him with a shock of surprise. He thenceforth led a double life—preparing and publishing in this world the stores of spiritual wisdom he had gathered in the other.

The case of this man is altogether unique in the

history of mankind. It presents very few points of resemblance to the case of any previous Seer, Reformer, or Spiritualist, in the world. It must be judged rather by its points of dissimilarity. The dignity of his demeanor was worthy of the grandeur of his mission. He made no pretensions, sought no discussions, attempted no conversions; but in sublime silence planted the seed of the new kingdom of God—that seed which is "less than all the seed that be in the earth; but when it is sown, it groweth up and becometh greater than all herbs, and shooteth out great branches, so that the fowls of the air may lodge under the shadow of it."

As there is no possible avenue into the spiritual world except through the spiritual body, so there is no way out of it back to earth except through the same medium. No spirit or angel can resume a material body, or appear in the natural world, in a form which reflects the light of our sun. They know nothing that transpires in this mundane sphere, except through the spirits of people in this world with whom they are consociated. They can be brought into such rapport with the spiritual body of a man living on earth, that they can read his thoughts and direct his motions; and if the man's spiritual senses are open at the same time, they can see through his eyes and hear through his ears what is transacting in this outer world.

This is the key to the fact, which at first blush appears so incredible, that Polheim, a celebrated Swedish minister and intimate friend of Swedenborg, witnessed the ceremonies of his own funeral. He was surprised, as all new-comers are in the other life, at finding himself alive and apparently in the same body; but when he looked through Swedenborg's eyes into the natural world and saw his own material body laid out in state, his amazement was extreme. He attended the burial of his own corpse, conversing on the way with Swedenborg concerning the ignorance and darkness of the church and the world about the true meaning of the resurrection from the dead.

One spirit, newly deceased, who was attending his own funeral, heard (through Swedenborg as a medium) the minister say, that the body of their departed friend would rise from his long sleep at the resurrection-day. He entreated Swedenborg to tell the audience that he had already risen from the dead, and that he was then and there present in a spiritual body. Had Swedenborg complied with the solicitation of his invisible companion, his announcement of the most beautiful truth would have been received with unbounded derision.

The good angels, breathing always a living atmosphere of peace and beauty, had little desire to turn away from it and peer through Swedenborg's eyes into the darkness of our disorderly world. They could not help seeing and hearing something which shocked or pained them. He once noticed some little boys fighting in the streets, the bystanders encouraging the combat — a disgusting spectacle common enough in our own age and country. The angels who witnessed it through his eyes, and sensed the spiritual sphere of hell which surrounded the scene, were filled with inexpressible distress and agitation.

The idea of spirits or departed friends gliding invisibly around us and watching our movements is a popular delusion. There are no ghosts, but such as are generated in weak, excited, or diseased brains, and projected outwardly as hallucinations. The spiritual and natural worlds do not pass insensibly into each other, like light into shade or heat into cold. They are utterly different in material. They are connected solely by correspondence; and no person in the spiritual world can see into this world, except through the eyes of some human being still living in it.

Our spiritual bodies may become visible in heaven. We may thus commune with spirits from other planets or worlds even beyond our solar system. If any of those spirits should be in rapport with some human being still living on those distant orbs, we might see through his eyes into his physical world also. Swedenborg thus saw spirits from some of our planets, and from some earths away off in the sidereal abysses. A chain of communicating mediums might thus be established from world to world and system to system, and sensation, thought, and affection transmitted along the line from one part of the universe to another.

Our traveler by open vision gives us some wonderful accounts, as might be expected, of God's creatures in those remote regions of space. They differ sometimes amazingly from us, so that they cannot understand or appreciate our peculiar modes of thought and feeling. One spirit from a very distant globe was brought into such rapport with Swedenborg that he looked through his eyes into the streets of a European city. The scene was so different from any thing that he had ever witnessed or imagined, and the sphere of it, in which evil predominated, was so revolting to him, that he fled away in terror.

Some cavilers have demanded why Swedenborg, when describing the spirits who came from Mars, Venus, Jupiter, and Saturn, did not go further and tell us something of the inhabitants of those more remote planets which astronomers had not discovered in his day. The answer probably is, that those vast orbs, so distant from the heat and light of the sun, are still undergoing the immense series of geological changes necessary to prepare them for the habitation of human beings, and that, therefore, no spirits have ever come from them.

We have not been too prolix, if we have succeeded in impressing on the reader's mind the importance, truth, and beauty of this doctrine of a spiritual body. It is the central, pivotal point of Swedenborg's grand system of Psychology. It has science, reason, and revelation to commend it. The only charge against it is its strangeness. View it in all its connections and relations, comparing it carefully with the Written Word:—the strangeness will disappear. You will discover that it was only the newness of that glorious Second Advent Idea, of which our Lord declared:

"Behold! I make all things new."

Some persons are startled at the statement, that the spiritual bodies of our little children who have left us, continue to grow until they attain the full stature of manhood and womanhood. They expect to meet the little creatures who died ten or twenty years ago, and find them the same small, dependent, imperfect beings. This idea has arisen, no doubt, from the belief that the soul or spirit will finally be reunited to the same material body which was laid in the grave; for we cannot imagine how a fully-grown and developed spirit can reanimate the form of a babe. When we cast behind us for ever that odious dead-weight on Christian progress —the doctrine of a fleshly resurrection—which Coleridge condemns as a gross Egyptian superstition, we may advance into clearer and purer light, and see the necessity and the rationality of the continued growth of the spiritual body.

Mothers, whose love for their infants is kept alive in their hearts by the memory of its objective manifestations, wish earnestly to see them again just as they were. They remember the sweet little face pressing itself gladly against the maternal bosom; the kisses which they showered on the pearl-white forehead; the delicate hands and feet, more beautifully tinted than ocean shells; the thousand graceful gestures, and the endearing sounds which make such ravishing music in the mother's heart.

Now all these precious little associations, which make up the identity of the child in the mind of the mother, never perish. It is one of the wonders of the other life, that our mental states are all rolled up like a vast map, which can be unrolled again, bringing back in its fullness every thought, affection and deed of our past existence. A still more wonderful thing follows. Those acts of memory there are not vague pictures of the imagination, or conceptive faculty, as they are here; but they may be projected outwardly, taking visible shape and scenic representation, accurately repeating everything that transpired.

A man can thus be made to reappear just as he was when a boy, or even a babe, with every most minute particular of form and dress. A panorama of our whole lives can thus be unrolled and presented for inspection, not as painting, but as statuary. These retrospections frequently take place, for the discovery of truth, for the identification of individuals, for instruction, and for uses connected with regeneration or judgment. Swedenborg tells of two brothers who had been alienated in the world, and whose misunderstandings were dissipated by both being brought back into their early states of life, when the old fountains of fraternal affection burst forth with indescribable sweetness and purity.

But these are retrospections; the law of the universe is progress. How selfish and cruel it would be for us to wish that our beautiful child of two summers should remain always a child of two summers; an imperfect, undeveloped, helpless being, unconscious of the myriad beauties of nature and art; untouched by the sweetest and holiest passions of the soul; unillumined by the splendors of ever-expanding thought; and unblessed by the glorious visions of God and immortality! What would be a painful, pitiable abortion in this world, would be still more so in the next. No. Every human being was created to attain the full measure of a man, which, as the Revelation assures us, is "that of an angel."

The spiritual body does not grow and is not nourished by the appropriation of such food as nourishes the natural body, but by the acquisition of truth and its corresponding goodness. A continual influx and efflux of natural substances keeps our material forms in proper condition. A similar influx and efflux of spiritual affections and thoughts sustains our spiritual bodies. Spirits have the senses of sight, hearing, smell, and touch, vastly more acute than man; but the sense of taste is almost nothing, it is so obscure. The tables of the other world are shadowy in comparison with ours. Delicate breads, aromal fruits, nectars, wines, and flowers: symbols of spiritual things rather than food. Their feasts are social gatherings, where Wisdom and Charity preside, and where the ideas and emotions of the happy guests are reproduced around them in graceful representative forms, as the souls of artists and poets are projected outwardly in painting and song.

The changes which the spiritual body undergoes after death are representative of the changes which are taking place in the soul itself. The child grows by becoming more rational, intelligent, and truly spiritual, until it attains the full development of man or woman; for angels, also, are male and female. Those who die in infancy always retain a fresh and youthful appearance; and those who die advanced in years, if they have lived on earth a life of charity, return to the freshness and bloom of early manhood or womanhood. There is a beautiful new infancy and childhood dormant, like a bird in the shell, in the old, wrinkled, and tottering forms of all such while in the flesh. Many persons, who are uninstructed in these matters, will be amazed to find the dear old grandmothers and grandfathers, who passed away from them with gray heads and wrinkled faces, transformed into beautiful and blooming beings in the prime of life! Spiritual time measures only the progress towards perfection, and has no ravages to display.

The spiritual body appears, immediately after its resurrection, the perfect image and counterpart of the natural body, from which it was extricated. Every imperfection in form, feature, speech, or motion is retained; for nothing ever existed in the natural body but by correspondence with something in the spiritual. So they are perfectly alike. The spiritual body is even for a time clad in the same kind of garments, to all appearance, which the man wore on earth—a fact which shows to the denizens of the other world that he is a new-comer from our own. He is not arrayed in the "fine linen" of the saints, until his interior life has been brought into perfect harmony with that of the saints.

The spiritual body begins changing with the removal or separation of the evil spheres, hereditary and acquired, which are so closely interwoven with our moral structures. These evil spheres are the sole causes of the Unbeautiful in man and nature, and of all the deviations from the perfect lines of beauty and order in the universe. As the spirit is gradually disentangled from these spheres by the wonderful processes of exploration, judgment, and instruction, which take place in the intermediate world of spirits, its progress is pictured in the improved and beautified state of its spiritual body. Every deformity or imperfection gradually disappears. Every line of care and sorrow is removed; every trace of passion or selfishness or sensuality is obliterated. The faces of some persons undergo such astonishing changes, that it is difficult at first for their nearest friends just coming into the spiritual world to recognize them. The faces of the angels become so extremely beautiful, with infinite variety, as to baffle all efforts at description.

By the same organic law of the spiritual world, that the exteriors and interiors shall correspond, those who grow in evil grow in ugliness and deformity. Evil spirits become terribly hideous in the light of heaven; but as their tastes are as perverted as their forms, they continue to think themselves models of beauty and wisdom.

Man, being a free agent, is capable of thinking

one thing and saying another; of feeling in one way, and pretending to feel in the opposite. This great sin of deceit has degraded the race for thousands of years, and transmitted its ever-increasing physical marks from father to son, until very few persons in the world can be said to have absolutely their own faces. The great judgment awaiting each individual directly after death will rectify all this, and beauty will be given only to those to whom beauty belongs.

"To grow old in heaven," says Swedenborg, "is to grow young." There is no permanent childhood there, nor old age, but only glorious manhood and womanhood. There is no autumn or winter, but only spring and summer. There is no night there, but only morning and evening. There is no heat there but the glow of Love; no light but the brightness of Truth. There is no God there but the Divine Man, our Lord Jesus Christ.

CHAPTER IV.

WHERE DO THEY GO?

IS it not wonderful that any human being, not actually insane, should have doubted the final salvation of infants and little children?

Read the beautiful teachings of our Lord himself on this subject:

"Suffer the little children to come unto me, and forbid them not; for of such is the kingdom of God."

"And He took a child and set him in the midst of them; and when He had taken him in his arms, He said unto them:

'Whosoever shall receive one of such children in my name, receiveth me.'"

"Take heed that ye despise not one of these little ones; for I say unto you that in heaven their angels do always behold the face of my Father which is in heaven."

"Verily I say unto you, Whosoever shall not receive the kingdom of God as a little child, shall in no wise enter therein."

"Even so, it is not the will of your Father which is in heaven, that one of these little ones should perish."

In the face of these teachings, the letter and spirit of which are so heavenly, the logical necessities of a false theology have driven some of its leaders in former times into the execrable doctrine, that there were infants and children in hell! The same logical necessities still exist; but the heart of humanity has outgrown its creed: no one believes it now.

We can imagine that in an age of great moral darkness, when persecution and torture for opposing religious opinions were considered acceptable to God, grave and learned divines might persuade themselves and even others, that there were myriads of infants in hell "not more than a span long." What shall we say when the great poet, the man with "the vision and faculty divine," loses his intuitive perception of truth, and describes the other life as it appears through the dark veil woven of ecclesiastical cobwebs?

Dante inscribed over the sombre arch of the gate to hell these awful words:

> "All hope abandon, ye who enter here."

On getting into the first circle of the infernal

realm, he reports the whole air tremulous with the eternal wails of a vast multitude of infants, who had never been baptized into the church. Oh, the cruel tyranny of the Religious Idea, when it reflects the unregenerate human heart and not the will of God!

From these dreamers, clerical and lay, let us turn to the testimony of the Seer, who describes so clearly and truthfully what he has heard and seen. "Heaven and its wonders, and Hell; from things heard and seen;" is the title of one of his books.

"I have been informed of a certainty that all infants who die throughout the whole world, are raised up by the Lord and conveyed into heaven; and are there educated and instructed by the angels who have the care of them; and also grow up to maturity as they advance in intelligence and wisdom. It may be seen, therefore, how immense the heaven of the Lord would be, if it were composed of little children only; for they are all instructed in the truths of faith and in the good things of mutual love, and become angels."

At what age, then, does moral responsibility begin? Are not many children fully sensible of the difference between right and wrong at a very early period? Many a parent's heart has been saddened by great clouds of fear and doubt on this subject. Some beautiful and intelligent child of ten or fifteen years, has been snatched away into the world of spirits without having made any special confession of sin, without repentance, without what is called "saving faith," without conversion.

Will such a child go to heaven, with all its little imperfections on its head? Sombre theologians look grave and are puzzled at the question. The pietistic books of the churches give no light, but excite suspicion and foster apprehension. The uncovenanted mercy of God is the forlorn hope. Thorns pierce the parental heart. Many cypress leaves are interwoven in the chaplet of roses which adorns the graves of such little ones.

The point acquires a still more painful interest, because the doubtful element is increased, when the victim of death is just verging into a radiant, happy, and hopeful manhood or womanhood. Overflowing with natural vivacity, eager for the gayeties, the pleasures, the business of the world, the young spirit is summoned away before it has acquired a full conception of the meaning of life or death; before the religious idea, as taught by the dominant theologies, has made any profound impression on the mind or heart. Without faith in Christ, without conviction, without a sense of justification, without interest in God or spiritual things, how can such a person be saved?

It is useless to institute comparisons of opinion where all alike are based, not upon experimental knowledge, but on theological subtleties of interpretation. Passing the authorities of the Old Church entirely by, we will consult the heart-cheering, soul-illuminating revelations of the New, thanking God for the light which has come into the world.

Swedenborg divides the moral states of our life into three stages. The first is one of innocence and ignorance, extending from birth to the age of five years. The second is the stage of instruction, or formation of the elements of character, reaching from five years to twenty. The third is the period of intelligence and rationality, extending from twenty to sixty, or to death. After sixty the tendency is to revert to the state of childhood again, with the character acquired or formed during life on earth as the basis of a new life in the spiritual world.

From five to twenty we are taught by masters, and think, not from and of ourselves, but under authority. The soul grows, as the body grows

We are appropriating and assimilating to ourselves, during that period, what we derive from others; from parents, nurses, teachers, companions. books, nature, society, &c. Not that which goes into a man defiles him; but that which is generated within him by his own voluntary powers, and proceeds from him as his own.

No one, according to what we love to call the "Heavenly Doctrines," is responsible for hereditary or original sin. That is a terrible burden we all bear, impelling us continually to violations of the moral law. We only suffer the penalty, however, of our own transgressions, and then only of those committed in states of liberty and rationality. No genuine reformation of character takes place in states of ignorance, insanity, sickness, or coercion, whether mental or physical. Therefore persons under twenty, or thereabouts, are not fully responsible, because they are not in states of liberty or rationality. They are not freed from the necessary mastership of other wills than their own; nor is the rational faculty fairly developed. There can be no genuine spiritual life until it is voluntarily sought after in a state of maturity, physical and psychological.

We may safely assume, that no one dying under

the age of twenty can be finally lost; for, no matter what may have been done in the flesh, it will be found, on the final adjustment, when all things are unraveled and made right, that there is yet enough spiritual ground to be created (not renovated but created—the soul, like the body, being imperfect), for heavenly influences still to prove triumphant.

There is authority from the letter of the Bible for this view of the matter. On account of the murmurings of the Hebrews against the Lord, the entire generation which came out of Egypt over twenty years of age, with the exception of Caleb and Joshua, were doomed to perish in the wilderness. Those under twenty were spared and permitted to enter the Holy Land, after a period of trial and temptation. They were exempted because they were not considered morally responsible for participating in the sins of their fathers.

We are not condemned for evils until we can discern, analyze, judge, and conclude for ourselves; and until, exercising our free will in a state of perfect rationality and freedom, we deliberately choose the evil way; nor does all hope of reformation and final salvation vanish, until we have obstinately confirmed ourselves in evil, and have resisted all the good influences which may be brought to bear upon us both in this world and in the world of spirits.

This explains why it is, as Swedenborg assures us, that so many of the heathen go to heaven. Their souls remain in an imperfect and childlike condition during this life; and they do not advance into states of true rationality and liberty until they enjoy or suffer the experiences of the spiritual world. The worst of all spirits come from Christendom,—a fact not very flattering to our boasted civilization; and the very lowest depth is assigned to those who have used the insignia of piety and the machinery of the Christian church, to foster their own ambition and self-love by acquiring spiritual dominion over the minds of men.

It is conceded, then, that all infants and children go to heaven.

Heaven! Beautiful, sweet, inspiring word! Is it imaginary, or is it because the Christian heart is so frequently and sweetly entranced in contemplation of these sacred themes, that it finds such a special, tender, musical charm in the words, love, goodness, innocence, peace, angels, home, heaven, and the Lord?

Where and what is Heaven?

An old English divine, who was asked whether

heaven was a state or a place, wisely answered, "A state first, and a place afterward." The Christian church is well acquainted with the meaning of the heavenly "state" as attained by the process of regeneration. It has made many ingenious speculations about the heavenly "place." Swedenborg explains to us, by divine authority, the true nature of both, and gives the key of correspondence which unfolds the organic connection existing between them.

What a strange idea of heaven it is, that our spirits will travel over illimitable spaces, upwards and outwards, far away beyond our visible universe, into some vast central Sun, where they will find the great city and the white throne and the jasper sea! As if a mere remove on the same plane, however great, from our present habitat, could deliver us from the bondage of time and space, and of these perishing material forms, and bring us face to face with the verities of the Lord's spiritual kingdom!

There is indeed a central Sun; but no straight or curved line drawn from our terrestrial bases will ever reach it. The old Chaldean oracles, fragments of angelic wisdom, speak of two Suns; and of one as "more true" than the other. That "more true" Sun shines throughout the entire spiritual universe, and its heat and light are the Love and Wisdom of the Divine Man, who is the Centre and Life of all things.

A spiritual universe surrounds and interpenetrates the entire physical universe. Within and around each planet there is a spiritual orb composed of spiritual substance and full of spiritual inhabitants. There are three series of these vast spiritual kingdoms, one above another; the first, second, and third heavens. They are all connected together and sustained by the same inflowing Divine Life. The physical universe is the basis or pedestal upon which the spiritual stands. It precedes it in development, and is "established for ever." Here and there from local causes a planet may be shattered or a star expire; but that vast webwork of solar systems and constellations of systems and belts of constellations—this physical universe—is immovable and imperishable.

Heaven is not in this direction or that; it is neither upward nor downward. The road to it is not measured by spaces nor estimated by times. Heaven is not a place to be discovered by research; nor a city which can be reached and entered by every one, although its gates of pearl stand open night and day. Its glory is invisible, its songs inaudible, its heights inaccessible, to all but those who bear in their bosoms the heavenly "state" which creates and reveals around them the heavenly "place."

How plainly does our Lord assure his disciples that heaven is neither here nor there, but *within* themselves. Flesh and blood cannot inherit the kingdom of God. The spiritual body alone can rise into heaven. To give a philosophical definition: Heaven is the Lord in the human soul; the Lord's love and wisdom appropriated and reappearing as affection and thought in the heart and brain, or in the will and understanding, of the regenerate man. When a man feels and thinks as the Lord would have him feel and think—when the Lord's will is done in the spirit, so that man is an image or likeness of God—he has heaven within him.

The heaven without and around the angels, the external heaven, the place which philosophers call "the objective," is created instantaneously and from moment to moment by the Lord, in perfect correspondence with the heaven within, or with the states of their affections and thoughts derived from the Lord. The causes are all within; the effects are all without. The outward and visible substances are plastic to the unseen operations of the spirit, taking forms and colors according to the secret changes of the soul

This law of correspondence between the internal and the external, the subjective and the objective, is the grand secret of creation; revealed to men in the golden age, and lost by sin and sensuality; concealed in all ages and countries in parables and fables and "dark sayings of old;" half discovered by poets and prophets in their finest frenzy; the key to the speech of angels and the Word of God; now restored again to an unbelieving world, by divine direction, through the agency of "the most unknown man" of modern times.

The angel's inner life is repeated in his outer world. According to his reception of the Lord's love and wisdom, the Sun of the spiritual world shines for him, near or remote; full blazing or belted with clouds; flaming with gold or gleaming with silver. His residence on mountain-tops or in valleys; in stately forests or by sounding seas; in silken tents, or wooden houses, or palaces of sparkling gems; his urban or rural home; his city, his temple, his associates, his raiment, his food, his amusements, his business,—all are outbirths or correspondences flowing from his own interior spiritual condition.

In that heavenly country, the flowers blossom and the birds sing responsive to angelic thoughts. Morning and evening come and go; spring and summer pass and return; not in obedience to a revolving globe, but representing the far more wonderful revolutions in the spiritual life of the soul itself. The world without him is a magic mirror, reproducing, as it were, in painting and statuary and music, the wonders of the world within.

We cannot here describe the form and quarters and times and spaces of heaven; the Sun there, and its heat and light; the mansions, the government, the worship; the temples, the writings, the marriages; the Word of God there; the speech of the angels; their power, their innocence, their peace, their wisdom, their occupations; the state of the rich and the poor there; of the wise and the simple; and of babes and little children. These precious treasures of knowledge are all contained in Swedenborg's "Heaven and Hell."

They will familiarize you with the world to come. They will open heaven to your understanding. They will enable you to follow your lost ones into the other life, and to realize in your delighted imagination the joy and the peace to which they have ascended. They will shed a halo of spiritual beauty around your life, and make you fearless of death. But if, in the fullness of your gratitude and the rapture of your enlightenment, you make a feast for your neighbors and friends, and call them to rejoice with you, and show them the great jewel you have discovered, stand prepared for the reception which the truth has ever suffered from the hands of those whom it came to bless! Some will fly from you like wild beasts when you offer them bread. Others will turn on you like swine trampling pearls beneath their feet. Some will mock you as visionary; others will pity you as insane. Some few will believe. Here and there some unquestioning Peter will leave his nets to follow you; some forlorn Magdalen will drop her tears at your feet.

It is difficult for those trained in the present sensuous or naturalistic philosophy to understand how the Lord's life is the life and soul of heaven. Our reception of the Lord's life determines the heaven within us and without us. There is no life but the Lord's. Men are organic forms, animated by inflowing forces from the spiritual world. No affections or thoughts originate in man. The Lord's life is an infinite current of Love and Wisdom, breaking, as it falls upon created forms, into multitudinous sprays of affection and thought. Man is simply the mirror which reflects the Lord's light, perfectly or imperfectly, according to his atomic arrangement, his organic constitution. He is a metal expanding under heat; a needle turning in the magnetic current; a mill-wheel impelled by forces independent of self. His self-will determines the reception of life from above, and the use made of it; but it creates nothing of its own.

All loves, with their infinite varieties of affections and delights, are derived from the love of the Lord to his creatures. The strongest and most beautiful of these derivatives are the conjugial love and the parental love. They are the fountain-heads of all the charities and graces of domestic and social life. The Lord's love of bestowing Himself in creation upon others, transplanted into man, becomes conjugial love; and his love of protecting and perpetuating what He has created, becomes our parental love. All other loves—the love of the neighbor, of relatives, of friends, of the church, of one's country; the love of knowledge, of art, of useful labor; every conceivable form of the passions and emotions of the human soul,—are simply finite manifestations of the Lord's one, loving, uncreated Life.

The analogue or correspondent of this great spiritual truth has been recently discovered in the natural sciences. The so-called forces of nature —mechanical motion, chemical affinity, heat, light, electricity, and magnetism—are so subject to similar laws, present such similar phenomena, and are so readily converted into each other, that philosophers have ventured on the sublime generalization, that there is One Fundamental Force, which becomes heat, light, electricity, motion, or affinity, according to its modifications in the atomic forms of different media.

The grand truth being recognized, that the Lord creates the spiritual world from moment to moment, according to the quantity and quality of his love and wisdom received and appropriated by the spiritual beings inhabiting it, some of the strangest statements in Swedenborg assume the most rational form. His details, indeed, are only intelligible from a knowledge of his largest facts or general principles.

We can understand now how heaven is separated from hell, and one part of heaven from another; how one man is organically in heaven, and another organically in hell, even while the fleshly veil hides from both their spiritual whereabouts. Evil spirits cannot see or hear anything in heaven; cannot even breathe its air. Not because the Lord excludes them from it, but because they have no good and true elements in themselves through which He can create a heaven around them. Angels of one heaven cannot pass to another, except through intermediate spirits; because their different degrees and qualities of interior life produce different exterior conditions. Every man's heaven or hell is the product of his own interior love and thought. His world is beautiful or hideous, according to the good or evil he has voluntarily woven into his own nature. A man's final state is not determined by any decree of Justice, but simply by the continued operation of the eternal laws of creation.

We can now understand the plan of salvation, the scheme of redemption, the road to heaven, the way to be saved.

And here, what shall we say of that scheme of redemption which has been taught in the Christian world since the foundation of the church; the angry Father, the interceding Son; the punishment of the innocent for the guilty; acceptance of the terms proposed, and imputation of righteousness after an act of the understanding alone? As no single element of this scheme is supported by the record of the Evangelists, or by even a hint from the Lord himself, what can we say, except to repeat the opinion of a great thinker, that the dark metaphysics of Paul has sadly obscured the beautiful simplicity of the Gospel?

Since heaven is the Lord's life in the human soul, the road to heaven, the way to be saved, is simply to receive the Lord's life into the heart. What is the Lord's life? It comes to our understandings as the Lord's Will—what He loves and wills to be done. But if the Lord's life works in us and through us perpetually, why is not his will done? Simply because we react against it. Let us cease to react against it; "cease to do evil," because He so commands us; because evil, or reacting against God, is sin; and the whole work is done,—at least all that we have to do or can do.

This is the reason why the commandments of the Lord are almost always negative. He does not command us to fast, to pray, to give alms, to attend church, to mortify ourselves, to make sacrifices of all sorts, or to believe any particular doctrine or creed. He merely commands us to abstain from idolatry, from image-worship, from murder, from adultery, from theft, from lying, from covetousness, from doing our own work on the Sabbath day.

There is a deep organic reason for these negative commands. We can never do any good thing so long as we resist or react against the Divine Will; and so soon as we abstain from evils of all kinds and permit the Lord to work in us and through us, get rid of the dominating influence of self, and open the door of the heart to divine influences, we discover that "there is none good but One, that is, God;" and that we are mediums through whom the divine goodness works, and not active agents, except in the mere sense of co-operation.

The old man with his lusts and the evil heart of stone are never changed into the new man and into the heart of flesh. The old man is simply thrust aside or displaced, and the new man—a new creature or creation—installed in his place. This new man is not ourself, but the Lord within us—the heaven within. The highest, brightest, and purest angel knows very well, that, independent of the Lord's presence within him, he is no better than the most utterly irreclaimable devil in hell. He would rebuke the imputation of goodness as Sir Launcelot did that of greatness:

> "In me there dwells
> No greatness, save it be a far-off touch
> Of greatness, to know well I am not great."

The true plan of salvation consists then in washing in the river Jordan seven times—that simple process recommended by Elisha to the conceited and angry leper. It is to remove evil things from our external man by refraining from doing evil. The Lord does all the rest. He enters our open doors and sups with us, as He promised. New life, new love, new aspirations pour upon us; not ours, but His. An increased love of the Lord, of the neighbor, of the Church, of the Word, of our country, of our friends, of our business, from which the old foul traces of self-love or selfishness are eliminated, is the sign and proof of His presence.

Self is the obstruction which keeps the Lord and heaven out of our hearts. When we surrender all our evil passions and false opinions—our pride, our folly, our contempt of others, our ambition, our prejudices, our restless endeavors to aggrandize ourselves in some manner; we find that there is no goodness or truth in us, but that we have been reduced to the state of childhood again. That is the meaning involved in our Lord's words, that unless we receive the kingdom of heaven as a little child, we cannot enter therein.

Children are interiorly and organically in heaven. Of course they all go to heaven, as we term it, when the external veil or fleshly body drops from them. They are in heaven, because they have formed and confirmed no moral and intellectual selfhood, but are open and plastic to the influence of heavenly forces. From birth to five years, they are attended by celestial angels; from five to twenty, by spiritual angels. These angels do all they can to break or modify the hereditary tendency to evil, and to prevent the formation of a selfish character.

This great truth, that we are spiritually born in heaven and descend from it to earth, losing our celestial and then our spiritual life as we recede from the great Source of all life, is beautifully stated by one of the purest poets of the world:

"The Soul that rises with us, our life's Star,
Hath had elsewhere its setting,
And cometh from afar;
Not in entire forgetfulness
And not in utter nakedness,
But trailing clouds of glory do we come
From God, who is our home.
Heaven lies about us in our infancy!
Shades of the prison-house begin to close
Upon the growing Boy,
But he beholds the light and whence it flows,
He sees it in his joy:

> The Youth, who daily farther from the East
> Must travel, still is Nature's Priest,
> And by the vision splendid
> Is on his way attended:
> At length the Man perceives it die away,
> And fade into the light of common day."

Heaven, though so near to us in one sense, is very far from us in another. Our sins have so separated us from the pure and beautiful natures of those who live in heaven, that very few human beings can pass at once from this world into the company of angels. This is true even of children, except little babes. The spirits of falsehood and selfishness, of envy, pride, jealousy, and cruelty, take early possession of our poor, fallen souls. Scarcely a little one five or ten years of age enters the bright portals of the Morning Land, without more or less of these spiritual stains upon its still undeveloped nature. We cannot pass at once from the dark and dense medium of earthly passion and thought, into the golden atmospheres of heavenly affections. These evil and false things which we imbibe, or which have unfolded from the awful depths of hereditary depravity, how are they removed?

The idea that some great and miraculous change takes place at death, by which the spirit is made perfectly pure and holy, and fitted instantaneously for heaven, has no foundation in reason or revelation. We rise from our natural bodies with every affection and appetite, every thought and opinion, we had entertained or contracted here. We are just as infirm and imperfect and impure after the resurrection as before it. We find ourselves in the world of spirits, the vast reservoir of all the departed, a state and its corresponding place intermediate betweeen heaven and hell.

This is Hades, the place of departed spirits; the place into which our Lord descended after his resurrection, and where He preached to the souls that were in prison. This is the paradise in which He met the spiritual form of the penitent thief who was crucified with Him on Calvary. The locality and uses of that world are most important elements in the spiritual history of our globe. In that world the souls of men were gathered at the time of our Lord's incarnation. A great Judgment took place there during His earthly life. The good and evil were separated; the old ceremonial system passed away, and a New Dispensation was inaugurated. A similar Judgment occurred in that world in 1757, and the germ of the Lord's Last and Everlasting Church, the New Jerusalem, was planted upon earth. No general Judgment will ever occur again; but each individual now passes immediately after death to the judgment.

This judgment is no great judicial process similar to those we have upon earth, by which guilt is detected and punishment decreed. The soul is freed from all external restraints, all bonds of law, custom, or authority, which bound it here; and is led into such societies and states, that its genuine, untrammeled, interior nature may come to the surface and be revealed to itself and to all others. It is not punished for any thing it has ever done. Its punishment comes only from itself. It is permitted to choose its own life, its own associates, its own place; and every one passes into heaven or hell of his own free choice. He is attracted hither or thither by profound spiritual affinities, and his inmost qualities continue to radiate forth into flowers and fruit—beautiful or ghastly, sweet or bitter—to eternity.

What surprise, and in some cases what horror, must strike Christians educated under the present system of thought, when they discover a few days after death, that they are wholly unfit for the society of angels; and that a great work of spiritual exploration and judgment awaits them; and that a thorough reconstruction must take place in their natures before they can reach their happy homes among the redeemed!

They are permitted, indeed, by the mediation of good spirits, to enter the gates of the New Jerusalem and to see the glory of the City; to confirm their faith, inspire their hopes, and satisfy a legitimate curiosity; but they cannot live there at once; and they are taken back to the world of spirits, to have all the secret evils of their hearts exposed and eradicated, and every false idea corrected and uprooted from their understandings. When they can feel and think in harmony with some angelic society, that is, in a spirit of perfect love and truth, free from all traces of self or earthly imperfection, they are admitted into that higher and holier sphere, and occupy the mansion which had been secretly preparing for them all the time by their heavenly Father.

Men remain a longer or shorter time in the world of spirits, according to the tenacity with which they cling to their evil affections and false opinions. It is sometimes difficult and painful to get rid of these foul incrustations of the earthly life. It takes a few months in some cases—ten, twenty, or even thirty years in others; but the good spirits and angels who labor to enlighten and purify our souls are blessed with infinite patience and sweetness of temper. Simple, uneducated persons and heathen, being more like little children, are taught and led much more easily than the learned and gifted, who have less real humility, more pride of opinion and self-reliance, and who have confirmed themselves by subtle reasonings in their mental states.

Is it not eminently rational that our spiritual character should be developed by these gradual changes? The proud, the covetous, the sensual, become humble and liberal and spiritual, not by any immediate grace of God, but by steady organic changes in the spiritual substance of their own souls. The evil and false things in us are as real as our flesh and blood; and they are removed, and good and true things take their places, just as the old material of our bodies is slowly eliminated and quietly replaced by new tissues and organs. A great deal of this work of regeneration is sometimes effected here, and the rest is completed in the world of spirits. If it be begun here at all—so much as the planting of a grain of mustard-seed—it will surely be perfected hereafter.

Children under twenty, and a great many adults among the heathen, not having had the rational faculty fully developed, have not confirmed themselves irremediably in evils and falsities. On the separation of evil spheres from them, the angelic presences within them pour down and outwards into life and action. The poor, little creatures, who were born and reared in the hot-beds of vice and crime in our great cities, are brought under the sweetest influences of education and culture. They are trained by good spirits until the filth and dirt of their natural life are washed away, and the spiritual diamonds concealed within begin to shine forth to the sight. Truly the sweet labors of philanthropy and charity are not terminated with our mortal career! What idea of heaven can he have, who has not already discovered and felt upon earth that it is heaven to do good to others!

Some children go to lower heavens; some to higher; some to very external societies; some to very interior; all according to their innate qualities and capacities. Each is sent to the precise point where his spiritual cultivation can be best effected. After they have passed from one sphere to a higher, if any thing false or evil crops out in the life, they are remanded back; nor can they advance again, until the evil has been thoroughly explored, confessed, repented of, and thus removed.

They are sometimes even let down from heaven into the world of spirits for further purification.

Little babes, having experienced nothing but a faint auroral trace of earthly existence, are conveyed at once to a certain, highest, inmost, and altogether indescribable and inconceivable infantile heaven, nearest to the Lord, and most immediately under his inspection. When they grow up to childhood, they pass down into the particular sphere or heaven,—celestial, spiritual, or natural,—for which they are organically fitted. They never have any conception of earthly things; have no ideas derived from time and space; think they were born in heaven; know no other Father but the Lord: and these are they whose spheres of innocence and peace are so powerful, that their mere presence can torment and disperse whole legions of evil spirits.

In the celestial light of these interesting revelations, may we not exclaim with the Apostle:

> "O Death! where is thy sting?
> O Grave! where is thy victory?"

CHAPTER V.

WHO TAKES CARE OF THEM?

WHAT confidence in the definiteness and fidelity of Swedenborg's revelations of the other life must they have, who seriously undertake to tell us something about those angels who receive and take care of our little ones when they die! Most people have so vague an idea of the other life, so little conception of its reality and substantiality, that they are quite surprised when told that the spiritual body of a little child just raised up into heaven, requires as much attention as its natural body did here. It must be fed and clothed; it must sleep; it must be trained to walk and talk. The little spirit must be instructed. A world of knowledge must be presented to it; a world of love must be lavished upon it. Who will discharge these tender duties?

Every child after its resurrection is consigned to the care of a female angel, whose ruling passion is the love of children; who feels more than the affection of any mortal mother for it; and whose supreme delight will be to make her little charge both wise and happy. There is no love, the mind incredulously retorts—there is no love like that of a mother, sweeter than life, stronger than death. Those who judge of our loves after death by their feeble manifestations before it, have formed no adequate conception of the beautiful expansion of heart and mind which awaits us all hereafter. If we shall then think with a brightness and rapidity now inconceivable, shall not our love, the first and deepest expression of our life, undergo also a proportionate increase?

Some uninstructed minds will revolt, also, at the idea of male and female angels. As if the grand distinction of sex could be obliterated by death!—a distinction which is universal, beginning with the Love and Wisdom of God, and running through heaven and earth, varying its forms but never its principles; through men and beasts and flowers, down to the married poles of every mineral atom! As if the grace, the beauty, the purity, the splendor of woman would not constitute the social charm and glory of heaven, as it does of earth! As if the passionate longing of youthful loves, each for the other, was not the golden dawn, the token, the prophecy, of sweet eternities of wedded bliss!

Swedenborg has satisfied the man of science, who seeks a key to the essential unity of form and function in the myriad-fold variations of shape and property in outward things. He satisfies the philosopher, who requires the true relation between cause and effect; and those great, pivotal, universal truths, around which all lesser truths revolve, like planets about the sun. He satisfies the theologian, who wishes to know how Jesus Christ is the Supreme God; and how His love and wisdom are the heat and light which vibrate through the spiritual ethers of the religious world. Does he satisfy the æsthetic soul, which longs to unveil the principles of Beauty, and to read the poetry of heaven in the stars, and in the flowers of earth? Only in part. Does he satisfy the frantic questionings of the inconsolable mother, bereaved of her child? Alas, no!

Had some noble mother, purified of earthly dross until her heart pulsated in unison with the golden ethers of some infantile heaven, been permitted to penetrate, as he did, the "far-folded mists and gleaming halls of morn," and, searching for her children, to gaze on the wonders and glories of the Celestial Kingdom, she would have told us things which would have filled the aching and hungry heart of maternity for ever!

Ah! But is the maternal heart of the present Christian world ready or worthy to receive such a revelation as that? If we have been faithless in our stewardship of a few things, how can we expect the Good Master to entrust his greatest treasures to our keeping?

Swedenborg, a wifeless and childless old man, was busied with the momentous mission of embodying in philosophic forms the spiritual doctrines of a New Church; not to be erected by himself among the institutions of men, but to be established by the Lord in the heart of the world. Teaching universal truths or general principles in bold, clear outlines of geometric beauty, he is frequently deficient in that minuteness and richness of detail, which we fancy would have added so much to the value and force of his revelations.

In the evolution of human literature, the poet comes first with his songs, preceding the philosopher with his problems, and the naturalist with his facts. In the opening of the heavens it will be different. A scientific and philosophic basis will be firmly laid, leaving little room for fancy or speculation. In the far futures, the Seers and the Seeresses of spiritual and celestial generations, may uplift veil after veil from still more interior heavens, and overwhelm us with their music and song.

Very much, however, that is both beautiful and consoling may be gleaned from Swedenborg in answer to the query we have propounded. We cannot learn the name of the good angel who has taken charge of our little ones. The new name written on the white stone, which she received from the Lord, is incommunicable to man. It involves her whole spiritual character, and that would be incomprehensible to us. Still, a little cheering approximation can be made towards a knowledge of its outlines. Even that will give us such a deep, sweet confidence in her supernal goodness and love! Preparing the way, we must explain first the true nature of the sphere of infants and little children, and the difference between the natural and the spiritual love of them.

The sphere of little children! What is a Sphere?

Every mineral, every flower, every animal, every human being, every spirit, every object, indeed, in the universe, from the sun to a dew-drop, has a peculiar atmosphere, composed of infinitesimal particles emanating from itself, embodying its interior nature and proceeding to a certain distance around it. We find it in the magnet, by its attraction; in the rose by its perfume; in man by his radiating influences of all kinds. By it the faithful dog tracks his master to incredible distances. By it the magnetized person detects the character of another by the glove or the ring he has worn. Every social circle, every church, every institution, has its sphere. The sphere of the sun is the creative force of nature. The sphere of the Lord is the Holy Spirit, which comes from or is "given" by the glorified and ascended Person of Jesus Christ.

The secret of our sympathies and antipathies lies in the nature of the spiritual spheres emanating from us. They are the antennæ of the soul, which we throw out around us to feel each other. Similar spheres attract; dissimilar spheres repel. Men and women, according to the goodness and truth in them, or their opposites, radiate forth upon others spiritual spheres pregnant with good or evil issues. The floral breath of vernal meadows and the reeking malaria of sultry swamps, are not more substantial than the spiritual spheres of men and women.

Imagine, then, the spiritual sphere emanating

from an infant! There is a brilliant halo about every little child. Happy is the man who can see and feel and love it! The old artists meant to portray it by the golden circle about the head of the infant Jesus. It comes forth in the serene light and beauty, the inexpressible repose, the innocent gladness, and the heavenly sweetness of the infantile face. It is discerned in the tender cooings and prattlings and merry laughter of their little voices; in their perfect forms, and in the delicacy and unconscious grace of every gesture and motion. Could we see and feel the full significance of this interior and exterior of infantile life, the hidden soul and its beautiful halo, every little babe leaping in its nurse's arms, or smiling in its cradle, would be as wonderful to us as an angel standing in the sun!

The causes of this infantile sphere are the states of innocence and peace in which their spirits exist—the total unconsciousness of sin or wrong, and the heavenly calm that flows from a perfect state of moral order and beauty. This innocence, and its consequent peace, is the Lord's inmost life in the soul. The more innocence and peace, the nearer to the Lord. Celestial angels—those nearest the Lord—are always present with infants and young children. It is the communication of their celestial sphere which gives to infancy its ineffable beauty and charm. The many-colored splendors of our little dew-drops on the earth are reflected from heavenly rainbows that are shining beyond and above them.

In the inmost or central part of every man's spirit there is a receptacle of the Lord's life. From that receptacle the life flows down into the organic structures of the soul, and becomes affection and thought, and finally action, according to the free determination of the spirit itself. Our selfhood reacts against that inflowing divine life. According to the force of this reaction we receive and exhibit much or little of the Lord's life in us. We may so shut it out that our life may be as unspiritual as that of the beasts. We may receive it so fully and freely as to be perfect in our finite sphere, as our Father in heaven is perfect.

The little child in whom no evil passions have been awakened, no false opinions formed, receives this life of the Lord without obstruction; and it shines through him, radiating outwards into the beautiful sphere of infancy. States of goodness and truth, inconceivable to our natural thoughts, are stored away in the minds of children. These are the basis of conscience, and the fountain and treasury whence all the virtues and graces flow out into action. They may be sadly wasted by continued perversion; they may be sealed and shut up, like magic caverns containing fabulous riches, the secret of whose entrance has been lost to man; but they can never be destroyed. There will always be a "remnant," the germ of a better nature, a chord which may be touched, a love which may be kindled;

"The bond which links us to the angels most,
The Light which may be hidden, but never can be lost."

The sphere of infancy is, then, a veritable Shekinah—an outward manifestation of the invisible glory of the Lord. The approach to the Lord is a strange way; not much known or thought of by the majority of people. It is not the aisles of gorgeous churches, trembling to solemn music and leading to gilded altars smoking with fragrant incense and glittering with lights and flowers. It is not the radiant avenue of the visible heavens, paved with stars, conducting to the ineffable splendors of a Central Sun. It is no spiritual highway, traversed by the strong-winged powers of the intellect, or by the swift-footed affections of the soul.

By no such ways can the Heavenly Father be approached. Who, by searching, can find out God?

No: The way to the Lord is nearer and simpler. Progress is made in it, not by prayers and fastings and almsgivings and ecstatic contemplations, but by merely ceasing to do evil; by putting away our lusts and falsities; by divesting ourselves of our selfish aims, our pride, our ambition, our self-reliance, our incredulities,—of almost everything which constitutes our boasted manhood; by getting emptied of self, and returning back, in some degree, into those states of innocence and peace which characterize the heart of childhood.

From this stand-point we can see the crystalline truth and beauty of the Lord's words: "Whosoever shall receive one of such children in my name, receiveth me." And again: "Verily I say unto you, whosoever shall not receive the kingdom of God as a little child, he shall not enter therein."

In that Celestial Kingdom, whence infancy derives its precious life, our Lord reigns; not as the King of Israel, or as the Lion of the tribe of Judah, but with the far more beautiful and endearing titles of the Lamb and the Prince of Peace. Qualities in the other life are frequently sensed as odors. Swedenborg perceived the sphere from the heavens of little children, as one might perceive the overpowering perfume of a grove of magnolias. He describes this sphere as making him feel "as if he were unable to contain himself, being seized and transported with such delight, that every delight belonging to this world appeared as nothing in comparison."

Not only is the Lord more intimately present in this infantile sphere than elsewhere, but this sphere is more powerful than all others. This is a paradox to those who expect to find the Lord in the whirlwind and the fire, rather than in the "still, small voice." Some one has said that a babe is the weakest and strongest of all things. Few have realized the fact, that all power, like life and love, is the Lord's alone. Therefore the sphere of Innocence, in which the Lord is most intimately present, is the sphere and seat of his highest power. From its serene height He governs all inferior things. Hence his government is perpetually one of Love.

No evil spirit can approach the sphere of innocence in which infants live, without suffering terrible tortures. An infant can put millions of devils to flight; and his continued presence in the infernal world would break up the foundations of its society and reduce it to a chaos of pain and madness. It was this sphere of innocence, flowing from the person of Jesus Christ, which made the devils cry out: "Art thou come hither to torment us?" "We know thee, who thou art, the Holy One of God!"

Hence the truth of Swedenborg's strange assertion, that evil spirits bear a special hatred towards infants and little children. They rave and rage at sight of them, like wild beasts in iron cages, burning yet impotent to seize and destroy. It is because they sense with frightful keenness the sphere of the Lord's innocence and peace emanating from them. The sphere of love, impinging upon the life-sphere of an evil one, produces hatred; the sphere of peace produces trouble; the sphere of joy produces pain. Thus evil becomes its own punishment.

Well may we shudder when we hear a man or a woman, and especially a woman, say thoughtlessly, "I hate children!" The least cultivated mind instinctively recoils from the thought as at the presence of something singularly unlovely. Where such a sentiment is real, which is not often the case, what is the cause of it? It is either some direful, perhaps hidden, evil of their own hearts taking verbal and symbolic expression; or it is some subtle, besieging, possessing devil who is speaking through them.

One of Swedenborg's clearest cut gems of truth is this: "The heavens love those who love children."

There is another beautiful statement made by him about the infantile sphere, which seems incredible at first sight, but is a necessary corollary from the facts he had already announced. Angels and good spirits, he says, perceive more intelligence and wisdom, more spiritual light, in the minds of very young children, when they read or repeat passages of the Holy Bible, or when they are saying the Lord's Prayer, than they do in the minds of adults. The children are themselves wholly unconscious of this great light in their interior minds. When angels gaze down into the mental operations of a Newton, a Byron, a Bonaparte, in their moments of profoundest reflection and study, they discover little else but flying clouds and darkness; but in the simple spirit of a small child, some little Charley conning his Sunday-school lesson, or some little Mary caressing her doll, they see the auroral lights, the glittering rainbows, and the diamond atmospheres which betoken the proximity of the Truth itself.

Why is this? The adult mind, by busying itself earnestly with the gross things of nature, by the cares and troubles of the world, by the indulgence of selfish and degrading passions and of groveling or ambitious thoughts, surrounds itself gradually with a dense sphere of selfhood, which repels the light of heaven. But in the beautiful Eden of the little child's heart, where no serpent has yet entered to persuade him that knowledge will make him equal to God: the innocence and peace of heaven abide; the glory and light of the eternal wisdom is shining; and the voice of Jehovah is heard in the garden.

This divine sphere of the love of children, which is derived from the Lord's love of protecting and perpetuating everything He has created, flowing down into our souls, becomes the spiritual love of children in our interior nature, and the natural love of children in our external life. It is vastly important to understand the connection and the difference between these two loves; and to understand that the natural love of children, divorced from its spiritual life and soul, is nothing more than the affection of animals for their young. Unless we know this, we can get no true conception of the inexpressible beauty and goodness of those heavenly

Shepherdesses, to whose care the Great Shepherd has assigned the little lambs which were taken from our folds.

Animals which have no spiritual nature, exhibit a love for their offspring as strongly as man, so long as their youth or helplessness demands the parental care. After that period, their parental love having no spiritual vitality, utterly perishes. The more cruel and fierce the animal, the more powerful and even terrible is its instinct for defending its young. The wolf, the bear, the tigress, manifest an intensity of maternal devotion which we do not see in our domestic creatures, because the will of the latter has been measurably subdued by their subjugation to man. The love of the animal for its young is purely selfish and temporary, and seems automatic rather than voluntary.

This selfish and merely natural love of children, divested of the spiritual element which enlarges and sanctifies it, is retained moreover by the devils in hell. Swedenborg tells of an evil spirit who was in a frenzy of impotent hate at the sight of a beautiful infant. He was told by some malicious spirit, and made to believe, that it was his own child. His animosity subsided in a moment, and he sprang forward to clasp it with an expression of the greatest tenderness. This touching scene was witnessed by the great Seer, that we might be duly impressed with the difference between a spiritual or heavenly and a natural or external love of children. The latter emotion, with all its apparent sweetness and gentleness, is capable of existing even in hell!

Many, perhaps most, earthly parents have only the natural love of their children. It is an extension of self-love. They love their own beauty, intellect, family, wealth, dignity, &c., in their children. They are proud of them as part of themselves. They are jealous of their growth; jealous of their love of others; and jealous of their departure from the parental influence and control. They esteem them for their brilliant accomplishments, their social fascinations, and their talent for acquiring money, position, and power. Purity of thought, charity of soul, sweetness of temper, the love of useful labor—those priceless crown-jewels of the spiritual life—have not been the burden of their parental prayers and aspirations.

There is a false spiritual love of children which frequently wears the livery of the true. Thinking about spiritual things, and thinking in a spiritual manner, may be two very different states of the thinking faculty. Many Christians think in the most grossly natural and even sensuous manner of the Trinity, the Atonement, the Resurrection, the Judgment, Regeneration, and, indeed, of almost all the great spiritual verities of our holy religion. So, also, interest in a child's spiritual welfare, a zealous concern for its manners, its morals, and its final salvation, may exist without any genuine spiritual love of the child. This seeming paradox can be made plain.

Not long ago, in the heart of the freest and most Christian country in the world, a minister of the Gospel of Christ whipped his own little child, for disobedient conduct, even to the awful extremity of death! Imagine a father bending over his own helpless, innocent little son, beating and beating, in violent passion, his head, his hands, his body, until with fright and pain the little mind becomes confused and delirious; he knows not what the father wants; hears not what he says; but suffers—suffers under the brutal blows, until nature gives way, and some weeping angel presses to her consoling bosom the little victim of the most horrible tragedy of modern times!

This extreme case, which is almost too hideous to contemplate, is typical. It is representative of much of the so-called spirituality of the age. This father excuses himself on the plea, that his intense affection for the spiritual welfare of his child led him unawares to the adoption of such extreme measures. Children must be taught obedience to parents—by kindness, if possible—by force, if necessary. Obedience, however, is the great spiritual necessity, and it must be secured at any price and at all hazards.

This dreadful fallacy pervades the reasonings of such people on many other subjects. The same anxiety for the supposed spiritual welfare of the church, the country, the neighbor, the family, is the cause of great trouble and sin in the world. It is frequently a subtle and diabolical form of selfishness—a lust of spiritual dominion over the minds of men. One may love himself supremely, in his opinions, in his patriotism, in his religion, in his family management, as well as in his business and his money. When one thinks that what he believes and does is altogether right, entertaining contempt for the opinions and conduct of others; that it his duty to enforce his principles and practice upon them in spite of their will; and that the end in view justifies the means used to attain it, let him beware! There is no true spirituality in his interior life; no true Christianity in his conduct. He bears in his heart the secret germs of all hatred, vindictiveness, cruelty, and murder.

This was once illustrated to Swedenborg by one of those curious symbolic visions which he found so pregnant with spiritual truth. He was infested all night by cruel and wicked spirits. He saw some parents combing the heads of their children with terrible saws, and lacerating their backs until they were covered with blood. The parents appeared simply eager to reform the manners and morals of the children. That picture represented the external or visible field of life. Then appeared a huge serpent coiled around a tree—his size was such as to inspire intense horror—representing their intellectual life, or the faith from which such conduct flowed. A third scene—some women carrying blackened pieces of human flesh towards a kitchen—symbolized the secret animus, the emotional life of such people.

He conjectured at first that these things were designed to represent the interior character of the cannibal tribes: but he was instructed that the lesson came nearer home to Christendom. It taught the interior character of those who are strong and bitter in faith, without the charity or neighborly love which is always the life and soul of a true faith. Such was the prevailing genius of his own age, and such predominates, also, in this—a little touched and softened by the approaching but unacknowledged light of a New Dispensation.

Swedenborg tells us, also, in this connection, that the least feeling of contempt or ill-will towards the neighbor contains hidden in its bosom such insensate hatred, as would impel one to feed voraciously on the blackened flesh of his enemy. This fearful analysis of the human heart is applicable to us all; for has not the weeping Prophet told us, that the human heart is "deceitful above all things, and desperately wicked?" When we would justify ourselves in conduct which violates the great law of mutual love, let us not be deceived; let us trace the real motive power up through the false reasonings of the intellect to the uncontrolled perversions of our moral nature.

What distrust, what fear, what pain, we should experience if we thought our little ones, gone from us, but not lost, were entrusted to the keeping of spirits or angels trained in our modern schools of thought! How enchanting the reflection, that their heavenly guardians have wrought into their own beautifu' lives the sweet lessons of the great Master, who blessed the little children upon earth, and who draws them into heaven; who taught us to forgive our enemy—not seven times only, but seventy times seven; whose thoughts are perfect peace, and whose laws are perfect love!

How then shall we distinguish the genuine spiritual love from the spurious?

Genuine spiritual love, beautifully described by the Apostle Paul under the name of charity, is invariably sweet and tender and gentle. It springs from innocence, meekness, and humility. It gives birth to patience, forbearance, forgiveness, and pity. It is the spirit of Christ and the test of Christianity. Whenever any thing austere, impatient, accusing, violent, or angry enters into our feelings and conduct, let us not deceive ourselves. We are the sport of devils. God's inflowing love has been perverted into hate. Our piety and philanthropy have the mark of the beast. Let us never forget that abstract truth or justice, separate and divorced in the human mind from the spirit of charity and mercy, is shorn of its divine and heavenly beauty, and becomes the minister of oppression and wrong.

We can now see more clearly what is meant by the spiritual love of little children. It is the love of childhood itself; a strong spiritual affinity for those heavenly states of innocence and peace which flow into the heart of children from the Lord. Interiorly it is the love of the Lord Himself as the supreme Source of all goodness and truth; of all innocence, all beauty, all peace.

This explains that curious statement of Swedenborg, repeated in several places, that the presence or sphere of an infant in the spiritual world is a sure test of the inmost quality of those who come within range of its power. He tells of a certain spirit who appeared to be an excellent Christian. He seemed kind and gentle and generous and humble. For a long time no evil could be detected in his character. When he was confronted, however, with a very beautiful infant, his secret animosity to the infantile sphere of innocence from the Lord was plainly revealed. On further exploration it was discovered that he entertained hatred towards many persons, even friends and benefactors. The veil of pretension was stripped from the subtle hypocrite, and like Judas he went to his own place.

Those who are blessed with the spiritual love of children do not love themselves, their family, their name, their possessions, their beauty, their intellect, in their children. They love the Lord, the church, the country, the neighbor, society, in each little infantile form. They regard them from a spiritual stand-point first, and from a natural stand-point afterwards. They receive them as precious little spirits, given by the Lord to add to the beauty and glory of his creation; to bring more of the sweet influences and harmonies of heaven to earth; to contribute to the order, happiness, and peace of society; to increase the strength, wisdom, and liberty of the country; to adorn, extend, and brighten the church upon earth; and to take their places, star after star, in the ever-increasing galaxies of angelic societies which constitute the Lord's kingdom in the heavens.

The parent who can fix these glorious destinies perpetually in his eye and ponder them in his heart, is capable of receiving the spiritual love of children. As we strive to realize those destinies by our individual regeneration, we shall approach nearer in spirit to those Blessed Ones who have charge of our beloved. We can measure that approach by changes in our own mental states. We shall entertain a profounder reverence for a beautiful and chaste conjugial love; and for the sacred responsibilities, sorrows, and duties of maternity. We shall feel a tenderer interest, a gentler care, a sweeter sympathy for every new breath of God, crystallizing itself into infantile form, even before it has emerged from the secret laboratories, where the Great Architect works unseen, laying the foundations of the intellectual earth, and spreading the curtains of the moral heavens.

It is impossible for us in the midst of all our earthly darkness, with all our selfishness, impatience, and folly, hereditary and acquired, fully to conceive of the infinite grace, strength, and beauty of this spiritual love of children in the heart of the angels. They have been purified from all mere worldly thoughts and emotions. Freed from the limitations of time and space, they have also been separated from every false and evil influence which harasses our world from the neighboring hells. They live in the clear, sweet, pure light of the love of God. They experience inexpressible joy in the sphere of innocence and peace which radiates from the little child. It is the first outflowering or symbolic expression of their love to the Lord.

This is true of all angels. It is true in a peculiar and extraordinary degree of those perfect and happy ones, to whom our children are given by the Lord to be reared immediately under his eye. Angels differ as men do; for angels are only men purified for heaven. Some are rulers, some teachers, some poets, some philosophers, some artists, and so forth, in endless variety. They are all led, under the Lord, by their ruling loves, of which there are innumerable genera and species; each star differing from another in glory. The ruling love is the very life, the essential purpose and passion of existence.

How inconceivably beautiful, pure, and holy, must they be in whose regenerate hearts the ruling passion is the love of little children! No spark of selfishness enters into this celestial fire. More or less of self is woven into all other emotions of the heart. Conjugial love is not free from it, for our eternal mate is a portion of ourself. We may love even the Lord for the sake of ourselves. But these beautiful Daughters of Zion, who live in the golden atmospheres of its highest mountains, love the little creatures committed to their care for the sake of the Lord!

These angel-mothers have generally been good and wise earthly mothers, who have passed through great tribulation to their final perfection. As their interior natures were unfolded by the revealing processes employed in the world of spirits, the love of infants and little children was discovered to be their ruling passion. They now live in the eternal delights of that heavenly emotion. Their thoughts are not troubled about the best means of training and education. They look to themselves for nothing. All the knowledge, intelligence, and wisdom, necessary for the perfect fulfillment of their duties flow immediately into their minds from the Lord himself. Nearest to the Divine Fountain, they draw the Water of Life in crystal cups, and the little ones who drink of it thirst no more for ever!

Children are assigned to these angel-mothers according to their interior characters with unerring accuracy. There is no guess-work, no failure, but perfect law and order, in the working of the social machinery of heaven. Each child goes to the very guardian best fitted to develop its good, to suppress its evil, and to promote its eternal happiness. These heavenly beings have no partialities, no impatience, no imperfections. They receive and love all children alike. Whether the little body has been drawn from imperial purple or a beggar's rags, makes no difference. No earthly shadows of rank or form or circumstance obscure their perfect vision. They stand in the place of Christ himself; receive his little ones in their arms; bless them in his name; and continually afterwards carry out his will in their loving care and instruction.

Compare this picture of the heavenly supervision of children with their state in this world; their bitter and cruel bondage; their neglect, their abuse, their sufferings, their sickness, their death; or, what is far worse, the evil examples, the false teaching, the early corruption, which so soon stamp their little faces with the cunning and sensuality of older natures!

O sorrowing parents! whose hearts still hang heavily, like drooping flowers turning towards the dust and the grave; who regard these glorious revelations with an almost total incredulity; or, at the best, with a mere flutter of hope that they may be true: may that same guiding Star which led the wise men to the spot where the Young Child was, lead you also at last to the discovery of your lost ones amidst the opening heavens and the songs of angels!

After your own resurrection and translation to the heavenly kingdom; when you can endure the splendors of the celestial sphere, and lift your eyes to the faces of those angel-mothers; when they restore to you your children—and such children! and show you how they have loved them, and what they have done for them; in the bursting love and gratitude of your hearts you will fall at their feet to worship, as the bewildered Seer of Patmos fell at the feet of the angel who had showed him the wonders of the Apocalypse!

CHAPTER VI.

WHAT ARE THEY DOING?

IN that sweet transition-hour between day and night, when the tumult of our earth-life subsides and recedes, and the heavenly life, which has always been present, although not always perceived, shines upon us again like the stars, the children come about us, and the soul reaches out eagerly after them with the old, inexpressible tenderness. We see them in the little chairs that are vacant; in the little swing that is idle; in the little books that are not opened; in the little toys that are not moved. We see them also in a better light than the feeble gleam of our natural memory. Peeping through the gates of pearl, we see them living, moving, growing, loving, in the Morning Land. We know they are not dead. We know it by the intuitions of our own souls whispering of immortality; by the promises of the Father; by the revelations of the Word; by the aspirations of faith; and by the songs of imperishable hope!

The forlorn maiden sits at this pensive hour on the yellow beach, gazing o'er the vast, blue waters of the cruel sea which separates her so widely from her lover. She wonders in what harbor his ship may lie; what he says and thinks and does; what scenes he beholds; what companions he is with; and she fears that the charms of that far-off Orient may encroach on the central place in his heart, which she claims as exclusively her own. So we, bereaved ones, stand on the shores of time, straining our eyes across the illimitable expanse, hoping to descry the purple mountains of the Celestial Country, asking our hearts the same eager questions, whilst imagination weaves her aerial tissues into a thousand shapes of beauty and joy.

We thank God that our lot has been cast in these latter times, when, in the fullness of his love and the order of his providence, He has been pleased to give us a clearer manifestation of Himself; to open for us the mysteries of his Holy Word; to reveal to us the true nature of the human soul, and the wonderful laws and phenomena of the life to come. What prophets and apostles desired to see; what poets and sages, half perceiving, have longed to verify; what the patient, suffering heart of mankind has yearned after for ages; has at length been unfolded. Imagination is henceforth needed, not to picture to us what might be, but to conceive clearly what is; not to give form to the hidden, but to understand the revealed.

We have already seen that our little ones have beautiful and substantial spiritual bodies, which grow and live in a heavenly world composed of purer substances than ours, but having the same general forms and appearances. The Sun shines there in the same altitude for ever; but it grows bright or dim to them according to their own changing spiritual states. There are mountains and valleys there, and forests and rivers with ever-varying forms and colors. The clouds move there as here, shepherded by the gentle winds; and all things outward are beautiful symbols of spiritual wonders flowing down from interior heavens, or from the Lord himself. There is morning, with its freshness and power; and evening, with its silence and stars. There is spring, with its silver and green; and summer, with its purple and gold. There are architecture and art and music and science; not as here, in their first buddings, but in their full flower and fruitage. And all these things are as real and solid to their perceptions as granite and diamond are to us.

We must remember this when we ask ourselves the question, What are our children doing in the spiritual world? We must not think of them as intangible shades, floating hither and thither in some inconceivable realm of similar shadows. Such absurd phantasies come of supposing that spirit must be something which possesses none of the properties of matter; no weight, no extension, no impenetrability, no color, no shape,—"sans everything." The fact is, that matter is totally inert and dead in itself, and has no properties. The sensations of weight, form, color, &c., are states of our own spiritual organization, which we ignorantly, but falsely, refer to our material world.

Little babes are given at once to their angel-mothers, who devote themselves earnestly to their care. They wash them, dress them, ornament them, amuse them, and by sports and songs and toys and lessons, and in a thousand ways unknown to us, give form and beauty to the dawning affections and thoughts of the little mind. Their language is at first composed wholly of vowel sounds, and, like music, represents only the emotions. Progress, however, in the evolution of thought is so rapid there, that in about a month of our time an infant will speak the angelic or spiritual language, of which the words are ideas, each containing innumerable things.

There is but one language in the spiritual world. All men understand that language now, for all men are spirits; but they have no consciousness of understanding it while in the natural body. When they leave this body they forget all human words, and enter at once on the universal speech, by which more ideas and thoughts can be conveyed in a few moments than by our earthly languages in a whole day. Children express themselves at once in this heavenly tongue according to their mental powers. We speak vainly of the rapidity of thought, and compare it to lightning; but we can have no conception in this world of the profundity of idea and felicity of expression of which even a child is capable in the next. How silly is the pride of our knowledge, the pomp of our wisdom! Our Lord Jesus, who saw into the heart of things, recognized in the hosannas of the little children, which so displeased the Chief Priests and Scribes, lyrics and epics of praise which never descended to human ears.

It may strike some as preposterous that we should possess the knowledge of a language, and yet have no consciousness of it in this life. Know ledge which is unknown seems a paradox. He has formed a poor conception of the human soul who thinks it has no operations but those which come to our external consciousness. The human body, which is the material image of the soul, tells, in anatomical language, the true story. We are conscious of its mere surface and of its voluntary external motions. The wonderful functions of the heart and lungs, and of the liver and other viscera; the incessant changes of the blood; the inconceivable vibrations of the nervous system, more astonishing than those of heat and light; all are going on within us from moment to moment without our feeling or knowing anything about them. Just so there are miracles of affection and thought transacting within our souls,—which are as truly organic forms as our bodies,—into the perception and knowledge of which we only come after the death and separation of our natural bodies.

Education, which is the communication of truths for perpetual application to life, is the chief business of heaven. It is carried to perfection there; for no evil passions spring out of the heart to obscure the understanding with thick-coming fallacies of all kinds. It is never finished; for it means the bringing forth or blossoming out from inexhaustible divine centres, of everything necessary to the spiritual life of man. We acquire new truths to eternity, and are made happy by using them as fast as acquired. The work is never complete, because the drawing forth or educing process is never ended. God's wisdom and our wisdom run in parabolic lines, for ever approaching, yet never to meet; and therein lies the secret of the happiness of heaven. The rest of the saints is the rest of congenial labor—of labor unthwarted and unsaddened by sin.

Every one is assigned his true place in that Kingdom of supreme order and peace. The interior nature of every child is inspected by the wisest angels; and he is sent into that quarter and given the very teachers and surrounded by the very influences best adapted to develop his peculiar faculties to the highest degree. There are no mistakes made there; no one is in the wrong place. There are no incapables, no self-seekers, no hypocrites. There is no dark and guileful soul there dwelling in imperial palaces; no beautiful and gentle spirit cowering in hovels and poverty. Neither kings nor people have any voice in the laws and government of heaven, except only as servants and stewards. The Lord alone is the Ruler; and the light of his eternal wisdom is for ever streaming down in swift judgment and execution, and assigning to each being, through his flaming ministers, his exact place and business and portion.

In heaven they educate the intellect by first educating the heart,—the true order, quite neglected in this world. All thought flows from affection just as light comes from heat. That Love begets Wisdom—the Father the Son—is the fundamental law of psychology. Such as the love or will is, such will the wisdom or understanding be. Pure and good affections beget genuine truths; evil passions beget all manner of falsities. Every untruth among men is the offspring of some evil emotion or appetite. Men abandon their prejudices and errors so slowly and with such pain, because they love them; because they have their roots deep down in their own affections.

In the spiritual world only the good can become wise. On this earth the intellect may be cultivated independently of the emotional nature. It may be vastly developed, even elevated into the light of heaven, whilst the will remains unregenerate and the affections and appetites are evil. But after death the affections govern supremely. The divine life flows into them first, and from and through them creates a correspondent intellectual world of ideas, thoughts, and expression. The understanding is thus the outbirth of the will.

This law of the spiritual world creates wonderful changes in the mental constitution of those who leave our sphere and undergo its impartial judgment. Many a learned man, many a philosopher, loaded with academic honors and boasting himself of his knowledge and memory, is stripped of every thing he had acquired. He becomes stupid and silly, and sometimes even insane. On the other hand many an ignorant and humble person finds himself suddenly filled with thoughts and ideas, such as no earthly education at present could furnish. The sole reason of the difference is, that one has received the divine love (which creates all things) into his heart, and the other has not. This great truth, that wisdom or true knowledge has no permanent existence independent of good affections, explains the mystical words of our Lord:

"Whosoever hath, to him shall be given; and whosoever hath not, from him shall be taken even that which he seemeth to have." (Luke viii. 18.)

It is easy to cultivate the affections of little children in heaven. Hell with its infesting spirits and terrible evils, is removed from them to the uttermost bounds of the universe. Its hateful spheres can never reach them. The earth-life with its limitations of time and space, its peculiar imperfections, its trials and sorrows, has been dropped like so much weighty ballast, and the happy spirits have soared away into atmospheres of ethereal light and beauty. They are surrounded by all that is good and pure and gentle, calculated to evoke the same qualities from the depths of their own souls. They never see or hear any thing that is false or mean, cruel or unpleasant; no quarrels or scoldings; no impatience, no fretfulness; no exhibitions of pride or vanity; no cunning or hypocrisy; no selfishness, no doubts or unbelief; no contempt of others. Oh, the sweet peace, the eternal calm, of the moral atmosphere of heaven!

Besides these negative advantages, they enjoy the positive and continuous influx of the heavenly spheres of innocence, peace, and love. Every angel about them loves his neighbors and companions better than himself, and the Lord supremely. Each finds his true happiness in exercising all his powers to promote the happiness of others. The result is a general social state of entire harmony and felicity. Such is heaven. And as these angelic loves are ever increasing in sweetness and power by daily fresh receptions of life from the Lord, the heavens are continually becoming more perfect and blessed.

Surrounded by such influences, our little ones imbibe the love of the Lord and the neighbor,—the ruling loves of heaven,—with great ease. They are trained so sweetly, so gently, so wisely, that their earthly faults and imperfections are soon removed; and after a short period no cloud of temper ever sullies again the serenity of their sky. They exhibit the tenderest respect and affection for their guardians, their nurses, and their little companions. The idea of self almost perishes with them, being reduced to the very last and lowest place. They grow daily in love, and in all the wonderful and beautiful knowledges that flow from love. Use to others becomes the guiding star of conduct—the dominating passion of life.

They are very early taught the mysteries of the Word in its internal senses. The highest angel in heaven acquires new perceptions of the divine love and wisdom when he explores the mind of a little child who is reading the Holy Scriptures. The genuine Word of God has always interior meanings, one within another, like concentric spheres. The spiritual key to that sense nearest to our human comprehension was revealed to Swedenborg. This key is the unfailing touchstone of Divine revelation. Whilst it unlocks the grandest spiritual truths from the Pentateuch, the Psalms, and the Prophets, from the Evangelists and the Apocalypse; it discovers that the Proverbs, and several minor books received into the Old Testament, and the Acts of the Apostles, and all the Epistles in the New, are only surface books, having no divine significance and no organic connection with angelic wisdom. They are the pious writings of good men, very useful to the external church here; but they are as unknown in heaven as the works of Calvin or Luther or Wesley.

Children are instructed in heaven by books and pictures and by oral lessons as upon earth, but with vastly more beauty, order, rapidity and perfection. They meet in magnificent buildings, glittering with jewels and pearls, corresponding to spiritual truths; or they walk with their teachers, engaging in intellectual discussions, through groves of inconceivable beauty full of music and ravishing odors. They are taught all our arts and sciences, and many totally unknown in this world. Earth at its best is but the shadow of heaven; and what we see here dimly, or not at all, will there be revealed to us in the splendor of heavenly light.

One method of objective teaching exists in that world which is impossible here; but the possibilities of that wonderful life would quite confound our feeble imaginations. Our artist toils long to cast his ideal upon canvas, or to shape it from marble, making it real; but the atoms of the spiritual atmospheres can be made by angelic volitions to take instantaneous shape and form expressive of the ideas in the mind. Historical scenes can thus be projected into outward form, and made to appear as if transacting before the eye. Swedenborg saw the resurrection of the Lord represented to children by this process with inexpressible tenderness and beauty, affecting the interiors of their susceptible minds with holy wonder and delight.

This process of projecting ideas into scenes and images apparently real, enables the angels to explore a man after death, so that his mind and memory can be literally turned inside out, that nothing hidden shall remain undiscovered. The murderer's crime, with all its horrible details, is said to be photographed on the optic nerve of the victim. That physical impression is transient. Impressions made, however, on our spiritual nerve-centres are indestructible, and may be called out ages afterward for our conviction. This is true of every word we have uttered, every deed we have done. In this manner all private and public history will be revealed and judged, and the truth on all subjects attained at last. Thus will "the Books" be opened.

Children soon discover that everything external in that world is produced by and represents something internal. The life of an angel is wrought out into his house, his furniture, his grounds, and into all the scenery about him. These outward objects are the outflowering of his spiritual nature into symbolic forms which represent his quality in every jot and tittle. They are peculiarly his, as a snail's shell is his, or as a man's body is his. In the other world, an angel's seat in the temple where he worships is so peculiarly his, that no other person can occupy it without producing confusion in the minds of all present.

The same law is illustrated also in every circumstance of their lives. The external reveals the internal. Their clothing, their ornaments, their toys, their chambers to the minutest particular, their gardens and every flower in them, are all representative of their own lives. When they have done or thought something wrong, a stain appears on their shining dresses, which cannot be concealed or effaced by artificial means; but when the fault is explained, confessed, and deplored, the corresponding stain disappears spontaneously as it came. When they neglect their prayers or reading the Word or any other duty, some beautiful article of dress vanishes from their wardrobes, or the flowers grow faint and dim in their little gardens. On the contrary, when they have excelled in goodness and duty, some new and exquisite piece of apparel or jewelry is produced for them, or their flowers bloom, as if smiling and approving, with heightened color, fragrance, and beauty.

So of every thing around them: it is symbolic and representative. The garlands and wreaths with which they are adorned, the medals and coins, the pictures and books with which they are rewarded, all report, in charming hieroglyphic language, the story of their moral and mental development. Nor are sports and games innumerable wanting, nor merry social gatherings, nor private and public exhibitions, to promote the general welfare, culture, and happiness of the swiftly expanding spirits.

Swedenborg frequently saw little children walking in beautiful gardens with their guardians and nurses, dressed in the most charming manner; whilst the atmosphere, the clouds, the foliage, the flowers, and every thing around them, underwent surprising changes of form and color, according to the changing thoughts and affections of the happy promenaders. So the flowers of Eden "gladlier grew" at the tendance of the beautiful Eve. Thus was exhibited to the life the groundwork of that hidden sympathy between man and nature, which runs in a golden vein through the sweetest songs of all the poets.

The increase of affection and thought is the business of the other life. Affection and thought are the meat and drink—the "daily bread" of spirits. They live from day to day by the fresh appropriation and assimilation of affections and thoughts from the Lord and from others, just as we do by the appropriation and assimilation of our material food. The hunger and thirst of that happy world is for knowledge and righteousness. No one busies himself there to get money or food or clothing or houses or lands; no one struggles for honors or office or position or power. Spirits who cannot be divested of such earthly passions and fantasies, do not go to heaven at all, but wander off into evil and selfish spheres, and stumble among the shadows and stone-heaps and pitfalls of the darker world.

Our children are taught by the angels to have no care or thought for external things; because they see that internal and spiritual things, goodness and wisdom with their myriads of genera and species, are the true cause and source of all objective appearances. Houses and furniture, food and clothing, wealth and power, office and honors, are all distributed gratis, in exact correspondence with the states of affection and thought which deserve and require them.

Has not our Lord said:

"Seek ye first the kingdom of God, and all these things shall be added unto you"?

This instantaneous creation, this appearance and disappearance of objects which seem solid and real to the senses, excites the stolid incredulity of our unilluminated natural mind. We expect to find these things in the Fairy Tales, and in such fictions as the Arabian Nights; but our modern self-reliant spirit, with its habit of scientific analysis and its sensuous philosophy, scouts all such narratives as the dreams of poets or visionaries. The true philosopher, the wise man, who distrusts his own powers entirely, and who despairs of any correct analysis, but follows the star of revelation that shines for ever in the East, discovers that these misunderstood fairy tales, mythologies, parables, Oriental stories, and "dark sayings of old," contain more spiritual truth and beauty than any moral or scientific disquisitions of our own times. They are fragments of primeval philosophy and wisdom, defaced and darkened indeed, yet "trailing clouds of glory" from the lost Edens of the race. This is the reason why they reverberate so sweetly in the souls and songs of poets, and fill the gentle, appreciative heart of childhood with such wonder and delight.

These curious laws of the spiritual world have been sometimes brought down into the natural world, in the special operations of Providence; and then, from our unfamiliarity with the causes, we call the result miraculous. The Israelites were fed forty years in the wilderness on manna, a species of sweet bread, which rained from the sky every day except the Sabbath. The oil and meal of the widow's house were daily renewed for several months. Our Lord also on two different occasions fed thousands of people on a few loaves and fishes. There is nothing in Fairy Tales or the Arabian Nights more incomprehensible or incredible than these things; and yet no Christian can deny oı escape them.

It was divine power, they say, specially exerted for certain purposes; and so it was. God's will, operating through spirit into matter, condensed or precipitated and rearranged the chemical atoms of the atmosphere into different solid matters. These cases illustrate what happens all the time in the spiritual world; for every thing there will seem at first miraculous to us. God's power is the only power there; and it creates from day to day, through the angelic minds, the entire universe which appears around them.

When our children are fully grown, they will enter on the duties of some office or occupation. It will be exactly the business for which they are best fitted, and in the prosecution of which they will be most happy. It will be something, the soul and life of which is to make others wiser and happier. Heaven is organized like the human body. Every atom works, not for itself, but for all others. It draws from the general reservoir what it needs for its sustenance and no more. The angels are incessantly busy but never tired. They take delight in the performance of uses. Their work, their amusements, their studies, their social pleas-

ves, move in eternal circles of beauty and peace, in which there is no sameness and no satiety.

They are for ever silently progressing in the regenerate life; for ever waking to a new sense of imperfection; for ever receiving new power and consolation from the Lord. No matter how good, how pure, how wise they become, the relation between the infinite and the finite is still unchanged. There are new worlds of Wisdom ahead of them; new Apocalypses of beauty awaiting them; new revelations of Love in store for them. Our hereditary evil, for which no man is responsible, except so far as he makes it his own by acting it out in the field of his own life, is made quiescent and powerless. It is there however, and it remains always as the groundwork of the contrast between good and evil, from which the keenest appreciation of the good arises.

Swedenborg saw a beautiful young angel in the third or highest heaven, who had left this earth when a very small infant. He belonged to one of the royal families in Europe. He had been reared in heaven, and was as near our ideal of loveliness and perfection as can be imagined. His external spiritual senses were laid asleep, just as our natural senses are in the mesmeric trance, and his inmost character from hereditary evil was allowed to come out to the surface and display itself in speech and gestures. It was found to be full of licentiousness and the spirit of domineering, the special traits of his ancestral line. When he was brought back to his conscious state, he knew nothing of what had been done, and was the same beautiful and heavenly being as before.

Thus it is with all men and angels; for all angels have been men, born on some material globe, and only escaping by death the limitations of time and space. Evil is the basis, the centre of our finite being, and everything good and true is superadded by the Lord—not acquired of ourselves, but given—and built up around it and concealing it for ever. So the land and the sea, with all their infinite varieties of beautiful forms, constitute but a thin crust of our globe, beneath which are fathomless pits of primeval darkness, sulphureous caverns which imprison volcanic forces, and vast oceans of central fire.

The angels, says the Word, are not pure in His sight.

So our children grow and live in heaven, inhabiting palaces of indescribable beauty; feeding on delicate fruits and nectars; clothed in shining raiment; sleeping without fear of any rude awakening, and drawing new life from the Lord in their sweet slumbers; associated with none but the wise and good; instructed by the most wonderful methods; enjoying the most delightful games and amusements; training under the wisest and best masters for positions of usefulness in the eternal life; developing mentally and morally beyond our poor human conception; attaining the full stature, beauty and perfection of the human form, and approaching continually nearer and nearer to that grander ideal, the image of God!

How beautiful is all this! how rational! how consoling! These revelations of Swedenborg are the sound of a trumpet, waking us up from the grave of our sensual nature, and inviting us to meet the Lord and his angels in the spiritual atmosphere of a New Life. The more closely they are studied, the brighter will be our vision, the more touching our consolations. Many things not explicitly declared can be logically deduced from the general laws and principles revealed. We thus acquire a pervading sense of the reality and proximity of the spiritual world. Doubts and fears are dissipated, difficulties are removed. Our thoughts are elevated and anchored above. Heaven becomes a world of substance and not of shadows. Hope verges into fruition; faith into sight. The grave becomes a myth. Life is a thing of beauty and joy for ever.

We cannot yet drop this enchanting theme. One other great event awaits our children in heaven, to make their characters perfect and their happiness complete. When they have attained the resurrection—that is, when they have put off everything selfish, imperfect, and earthly; everything which the inhabitants of that living world call dead; when they have reached the goal of angelic development, and are "as the angels"—they enter, male and female, into that blissful and eternal union, which our Lord could not describe to the gross and sensual ears around him except by a negation,—so widely does it differ from the "marriage and giving in marriage" of this world.

Man was created male and female "in the beginning," which always involves the end. He was also created in the image and likeness of God. The great elements of the divine nature, Love and Wisdom, which are mystically united in the Divine Being, were so separated and distributed in his finite creatures, that their eternal attraction, each for the other, should be the source of immeasurable felicity to intelligent and loving beings. Such is the origin of sex.

Woman is the special form of Love, man of Wisdom. Not that woman is devoid of wisdom, or man of love; but the relative arrangement of these great principles is different in the sexes. Each is the total outward expression of the other's interior life. There is the whole secret. Each was created for the other; is the other's complement. Each yearns, therefore, for the other with inexpressible longings. Man alone is not the image of God, nor woman alone; but man and woman so conjoined in affection and thought, as under two forms to constitute one being. This is the heavenly marriage, into which enter those only who have attained the spiritual resurrection, and have become as the angels of God. This marriage awaits our children.

These spiritual germs, created apart, are destined for each other and brought together by the Divine Providence; sometimes in this world, sometimes in the world of spirits; sometimes not until both parties have entered the heavenly sphere. They are prepared for the eternal union by all the experiences of this life, bitter enough sometimes, but bearing rich seed in their bosoms.

The preparation is continued by the unfolding and purifying processes in the other world. When all other loves have fallen into the far back-ground; when each is beyond doubt the other's final and perfect ideal; when they have become so thoroughly and interiorly harmonic that they feel and think simultaneously; when they are as fully one soul as if only one heart and brain animated the two bodies; then they are formally united by beautiful ceremonies, which Swedenborg was occasionally permitted to witness. They afterwards live always in the same house, in the same society. They appear at a distance as one man, and their happy spirits run in the same golden grooves of affection and thought for ever.

No priest officiates, for the church does not unite them. There is no seeking or giving away as here on earth. The process is organic and inevitable, like birth or death. It is like the blossoming of some beautiful flower after a century of silent preparation. The Lord works unseen. No one arranges or assists or can prevent it. It occurs in the fullness of its time, and men celebrate the event with music and dances and feasting. The social feast, and the formal assent of parties and the wedded kiss, are signs or signals that the Lord's work is done; that another angel, two in one has been born into the conjugial sphere of the Lord's Kingdom. That kind of work is never undone. That kind of birth is eternal life.

Swedenborg on one occasion attended in spirit a charming reception given to their friends by a newly wedded pair. How faintly we poor sin-blinded mortals can imagine the ineffable beauty, splendor, peace and chastity of those heavenly gatherings. The angel who stood at the gate of the floral garden in which this new Adam and Eve received their visitors, admitted none into that bridal Eden but those who bore on their faces the holy peace of conjugial love.

Happy are they who have ascended to heaven before their spirits were tainted by the impurities of earth; who have grown and lived and loved in those radiant atmospheres of peace and joy; who have never known any actual sin, and whose hereditary evils have been buried in eternal torpor; whose affections are represented by the lamb and the dove, and the naked infant garlanded with flowers; whose thoughts are reflected in the green pastures and the still waters that lie in the light of golden ethers for ever; whose love has experienced no rebuffs, no changes, no storms; who have never imagined that anything cold or unfaithful or discordant could ever cast its shadows on a wedded soul, and whose torch of conjugial consecration is renewed morn after morn at that great Sun of the spiritual world, which is the altar of the Lord!

A faint breath of that conjugial sphere is sometimes wafted downwards and felt perceptibly in the human heart. It comes in the shape of "love's young dream." It fires the soul with noble aspirations; it lights up the imagination with beautiful ideals; it softens the affections into inexpressible tenderness; it transforms the whole being with its ravishing sweetness; and shining forth into nature, it colors the mountains and meadows of earth with the gold and purple tints of the Celestial Morning. Music and poetry struggle in vain to give it expression; but it dies away amid the fast-coming cares and sorrows of life, and is remembered only as a beautiful dream.

That dream, gentle reader! was a voice from the spiritual world, prophesying the transcendent realities of conjugial love. It will return to you with thousand-fold intensification, and it will then be the life of heaven.

* * * * *

Beloved and beautiful Children! who left us in

such agony and darkness on those terrible nights, without a word of farewell or a receding kiss from your little hands, we know it is well with you, and that you are more beautiful and happy than ever. And we thank our good Lord for being enabled to follow you with the strong eye of faith into the world of light and glory. But, oh that the veil could be lifted for a moment; that you could leave your shining height and penetrate our world of shadows; that you could appear in this poor little room in which you used to play, we thought contentedly, and stand smiling on us by this little table at which you used to study, and which, with bowed heads, we have so often moistened with our tears!

CHAPTER VII.

CAN WE COMMUNICATE?

THE Seneca Indians had a touching custom of taking beautiful little birds to the graves of their friends, loading them with kisses, caresses, and messages of love, and letting them fly away into the blue sky. Such little birds are the winged aspirations of our hearts, which are daily and hourly soaring away in quest of our lost ones. Fruitless errand! Little doves are they from the closed and drifting Ark of our souls, returning only to ourselves!

Alas! that man, the Spirit, the only spiritual creature on the globe, should have his eyes and ears so closed to the Inner World, that in his darkness and sorrow he can only communicate the passionate longings of his heart to a bird, or a star, or the invisible winds!

If there is indeed a spiritual world; if our own thoughts and affections move and live in it; if our dear friends are there, loving us as before; if indeed, spiritual affinities and attractions cause proximity and presence; why do we not receive some token, some little sign? hear the fall of some footstep on the other side? or see the waving of a remembered hand?

Watchmen of Zion! who study the providences of heaven: Pastors of Christ! who feed his sheep and his lambs: give us light; explain these mysteries; satisfy our hearts and minds. Why are these two worlds so closely woven and yet so widely separated? so near and yet so far? How could an angel call "out of heaven" to Hagar in the wilderness, and yet no angel answers the perishing Hagars in the darker wilderness of our spiritual life?

We ask you for bread: you have given us stones.

Swedenborg's spiritual experiences, so prolonged, so thorough; undergone by one so pure, so faithful, so capable; granted especially by the Lord to illumine what was dark before, and to give a new doctrinal basis to a New Church,—offer us the best, the only solution of these difficulties.

Swedenborg declares that sin and evil alone have closed the avenues between heaven and earth. Wherever there has been no sin, there is open communication between the natural and the spiritual spheres of life. Our world presents one of the painful exceptions to this general law and order of the universe. Even here, in the times before the flood, the golden age of the poets, angels and good spirits were in daily communication with the inhabitants of earth.

Spiritual death, absence from God and angels, the loss of goodness and truth which alone really live, is the penalty of sin. Natural death was always a necessary event on every physical globe. All created beings are first born in this lowest or natural sphere, and ascend from it, by dropping the material body, into higher and purer regions of life. It was never designed that man should live on the terrestrial plane for ever; nor that having once escaped its bondage, he should ever return to it again.

How different, however, was death in that golden age from death in our sorrowful age of mingled iron and clay! Then every human being attained the ripe fullness of earthly life. There was no trace of disease, no infirmity, no suffering. When every thing was prepared for the change, a band of angels, relatives and friends, came for the happy spirit about to be released. They were visible to all around. Their presence was announced by heavenly music, aromatic odors, and golden lights The old man passed out of his now useless natural body as softly as a bird or a butterfly out of the little shells which had encased them. All witnessed the beautiful translation; and the troop passed away to their spiritual homes 'mid hymnings and blessings and adorations. The newly-raised spirit, growing ever younger and more beautiful, revisited day by day the dear ones he had left on earth, and cast upon their hearts and homes the consoling light of heaven.

The secret of the possibility of such communication is to be found in the inmost harmony of thought and affection which existed between the inhabitants of both worlds at that period. The men of that age loved the Lord supremely and the neighbor as themselves. Each person found his own true happiness in promoting the happiness of others. No one cared for riches or power or honors or the gratification of the senses. An extreme simplicity and purity of life prevailed. Our base appetites and unruly passions, our pride and envy and contempt for others, were all unknown. They took no thought or care for outward things. They beheld in the external world, as in a wonderful mirror, the spiritual mysteries which all outward objects involve and represent. This glorious and heavenly state of life has been so utterly lost to mankind, that we regard its story as a myth, a tradition, a dream!

Man gradually receded from those primal heights of goodness and peace. He began to attribute his riches of affection and thought to himself and not to the Lord. He soon loved the Lord less and the world more; the neighbor less and himself more. An evil state of heart and mind came creeping in, and was communicated from father to son. Men began to acquire property, to aggrandize themselves at the expense of others, to seek power over others, to despise others in comparison with themselves; and thence came, with accumulating hereditary additions, the awful lusts of the human heart and the hideous falsities of the human mind, which the wisdom and mercy of God through his revealed Word, his own Incarnation, and his established churches, have been able only partially to subdue.

It was impossible for angels or good spirits to keep up the sweet communion of the olden times. Angels can have no conscious presence except with good affections and true thoughts. When a man's end in life is the acquisition of riches or power or position for himself and his children; when his views are low, sordid, and selfish; when his sensual appetites have the mastery of his spiritual nature; the interiors of his spirit are closed. Angels are strangers to all such motives and sentiments, and are repelled powerfully from those who entertain them.

It is not only impossible for such a man to see angels or spirits, but he loses faith in their existence. He doubts whether there is any heaven or hell. The very being of a God becomes with him a matter of question. In this dark and pitiable state of mind, he believes himself superior to others in knowledge and sagacity. He prides himself especially on his logical powers and his scientific attainments. He looks down with surprise or derision upon those in whom the love of God and faith in the Invisible still survive.

It was the divine mercy which closed the avenue between the two worlds. The evil states of men not only repelled the angels, but they invited the devils to a more intimate association. Heaven receded, but hell approached. The world of spirits was full of wicked men, who came from the earth, leaving nothing behind them but their material bodies—bringing all their wickedness with them, and now doubly capable of inflicting the deepest spiritual injury on those who were left behind. The Sacred Word describes the effect on human society:

"The wickedness of man was great in the earth, and every imagination of the thoughts of his heart was only evil continually."

Earth and hell were becoming blended in monstrous union. Evil spirits took possession of the souls and bodies of men. Then occurred that great catastrophe, described symbolically as a flood, by which the spiritual life of man was suffocated, just as men are drowned in the water. The avenues between the inner and outer worlds were closed. A "remnant" was saved; open intercourse ceased; a new order of life was established; and a written Word and an external church became necessary to connect the spirit of man with the Lord and with heaven.

Since that period there have been occasional and partial openings. Prophets and Apostles, Seers and Saints, in all ages and countries, have had glimpses of the Holy City, and have communicated to their peoples spiritual light, varying in degree and intensity, but enough to keep alive in the heart of the world a sincere faith in angels and devils and a life after death.

Why cannot the intercourse with the spiritual world be now restored and resumed? What is to hinder us from having our eyes and ears now opened, so that we may test for ourselves the truth of what our Prophets and Seers have told us? Are there not intimations loud and clear throughout the world, that this glorious event is about to take place? Need we despair of seeing and conversing, before we die, with those precious ones who have gone before us?

To answer these questions rationally, we must first consider what is going on in that world of spirits which is nearest to our own, and which we would first enter, or see into, if permitted.

That world is a shifting scene; a world of judgment, of change, of coming and going. Nothing there is fixed. Two powerful currents of life run through that world; one setting strongly towards heaven, the other towards hell. Those who are preparing for heaven are daily receding farther and farther from our earth; because they are putting off their earthly modes or states of thought and feeling, and becoming more and more like the angels. They are being instructed in spiritual things; they are unlearning or forgetting natural things. They cannot come back to us any more than the fruit can return into the form of a bud. It would be painful, it would be injurious to their spiritual natures, to take so many backward steps to be brought into rapport with us. No: we can go to them by making the same spiritual progress forwards; we should not wish them to be brought back to us.

On the other hand, those who compose the downward current are being divested of what little truth and good they have ever had, and are preparing for hell. They are becoming more and more earthly, gross and sensual. They have a powerful tendency to return into this world. That being impossible, they gravitate, as it were, into the evil atmospheres of our spiritual life, and attempt to take possession of us. They are anxious to communicate with us; to knock on tables and attract our attention; to write through our hands and teach us; to compel our belief; to control our thoughts. They have all our own gross appetites and passions; more than our own falsities and errors. Operating, however, from the spiritual side, they may be inconceivably subtle, cunning, and dangerous.

We are not ready in this world for the instructions, purifications, and judgments, which are effected in the world of spirits. They come to us only after death. Nothing could be more disastrous to our spiritual life than to have the light of that world suddenly poured upon us here. We have our earth-work to do until we are called to go up higher—work of infinite importance to our own hereafter; and we should be unfitted for our uses in this world if we were living consciously in the other.

Swedenborg, indeed, lived that double life; but it was his special mission, and he was prepared for it and protected in it by the Lord. His Diary is full of accounts of terrible assaults and infestations of evil spirits, which certainly would have overwhelmed any human being less favorably situated. He has made for us, in a far more perfect and philosophical manner than we could, the very researches we so ardently desire to conduct for ourselves. His evidence is invaluable; it is sufficient; it is satisfactory.

A hundred years before the modern Spiritual Manifestations, and long before Mesmerism and its higher phenomena were discovered, Swedenborg was familiar, by personal experience, with all the sounds, sight, movements, writings, and revelations reported by modern "mediums." Nothing escaped him, from the mere displacement of material articles to the most astounding optical phenomena recorded by Home or Andrew Jackson Davis. He takes a view of all these things from the interior. He gives the true solution of the phenomena. He exposes the tricks, the fantasies, the subtle pretensions of these obsessing spirits. He describes their character with great fidelity. Most of them, he intimates, are great talkers and babblers, pretending to be angels of light, whose communications, full of sound and a show of knowledge, lead to nothing useful, true, or good; and their secret ambition is to teach and lead men in their own way, independently of the Lord and the Word.

At every period of remarkable spiritual opening, the evil rushes in from the other world as well as the good. When our Lord was on earth in a physical form, the same kind of spirits possessed the bodies of men in a manner incomprehensible to our natural thought, and His redeeming love was signally manifested in casting them out. So now, when He has come again in great power and glory, through a manifestation of spiritual truth, these evil spirits reappear, and on a new plane and in a different manner attempt to acquire their coveted supremacy over the human race.

Swedenborg impresses upon us, in the most powerful manner, the danger of open intercourse with spirits. Not only is there danger of being taught all kinds of false doctrines, but of being led into evils of life, which will endanger the salvation of the soul. When a man's mind is laid open to spirits, they enter into the whole of his external memory. They know his character, his thoughts, his wishes, better than he does himself. They can make him think and believe what they please. They can confirm him in all his errors of opinion, and impress upon him the most incredible falsities.

The vast majority of spiritual communications are utter delusions, the information of the medium not extending a hair's breadth beyond the natural range of our spiritual forces.

To illustrate: Some poor mourner visits one of the mediums to receive a message from a lost friend. The medium consents. The spirit proceeds to describe the deceased person with the utmost accuracy. Incidents are recalled which have been long forgotten by the applicant himself. The medium will write something on paper in the well-known handwriting of the lost friend. There is no mistaking it. If the questioner shakes hand with the medium, he will feel exactly the remembered pressure of his friend's hand, distinguishable from all others. He then delivers some message about family matters, indicating a most unexpected acquaintance with the business of other people. The inquirer is confounded. His conviction is forced. It seems a miracle, or a veritable communication from his deceased friend.

Now to one familiar with the laws and phenomena of the spiritual world, as revealed through Swedenborg, this evidence is altogether inconclusive. The spirit acting through the medium may never have seen the deceased person or heard of him. The latter may be away off in heaven and know nothing whatever of the trick imposed on his earthly friend. The spirit who actuates the medium has entered the natural memory of the questioner, and reproduced everything from its recesses. If he could make himself visible to the natural eye, he might assume the exact form of the deceased individual, so that escape from his deception would be impossible.

A more astounding case may be proposed. If your spiritual eyes were opened, your chamber might be suddenly illumined with magical lights of gold and purple. In the midst of them a glorious angel might appear, with the face of the Apostle John, radiant with holy love. He might speak to you in accents which would melt you to tears, and waving his wand, might show you the scenery of heaven; palaces of precious stones; groves of inconceivable beauty, and many of your own deceased friends walking about in shining robes and beckoning you thither. You would be enraptured at the sight, ready to believe anything your professed angel might tell you, or even to fall at his feet and worship.

Your visitor might all the time be an evil spirit, preparing to plant the most dangerous fallacies in your mind, and to lead you secretly on to your spiritual death. He has produced a fantastic vision, apparently real, by a magical art well known in the evil world. Wicked spirits thus infest and torture each other by all kinds of fantastic creations. These things are exemplified in the mesmeric sleep, when the mesmerized person sees whatever the operator chooses to conjure up in his mind—an immense serpent, a burning house, a sinking ship, or a scene of murder—the victim betraying plainly, by his strong emotions, that he thinks everything is real, and cannot break the spell which has bound him.

The vast possibility of spiritual injury from open intercourse may be surmised from these two illustrations. Spirits may personate our nearest and dearest friends, or those whose words have the greatest authority over our minds—Calvin or Luther or Wesley or Swedenborg. They may lead us subtly into pernicious doctrines. They may play upon our passions and prejudices as they please. They may inflate us with the idea that we have been chosen for missions of vast importance. They may start us on the most foolish enterprises, ending in ruin. They may poison our minds against our bosom friends; husband against wife, and wife against husband. They may wreck the peace of families, break the silver chords of reason, and impel to murder and suicide. All of this, indeed, they *have* repeatedly done.

But will not the swift-descending angels also come down and protect us from these infestations of evil spirits? Why cannot more good than evil come of these manifestations? Will not Divine Providence overrule every thing for benignant ends? Undoubtedly; but it is necessary to remember that all great organic changes in the spiritual as well as in the natural world, are slow in progress, and the true meaning of them cannot be seen at once. A change in the relations between the two worlds is impending; indeed it is already begun. It is the hope of the future, and the basis for the restoration of all things and the return of the golden age.

Nevertheless the first phenomena will be misunderstood and misinterpreted, unless men are armed and prepared with true spiritual doctrines to analyze and give them their right value and significance. When the doors are partially opened or the veil removed, the heaviest and lowest portions gravitate downward; and we have a deluge of vague, trifling, commonplace communications. Some of these probably come from good and simple spirits really anxious to communicate with their earthly friends. The majority of them, however, belong to the classes described above. Angels and good spirits can only appear through men who are as angelic and good as themselves. The heaven above us will only come down into the heaven within us. The "open heavens" will be connected interiorly with the Lord's New and Everlasting Church, the New Jerusalem.

The Lord meanwhile will hold the evil in check

so far as may consist with the free agency of man, and all the latent good possible will be deduced from it by the Divine Providence. Already these spiritual infestations have convinced millions of the reality and proximity of the spiritual world,—facts in great danger of being lost to mankind between the scornful denials of the skeptical element on one side, and the cold abstractions of the Christian Church on the other. They will also prepare the way for the reception of the authorized disclosures of Swedenborg as nothing else could ever have done.

These spiritual manifestations will increase in extent, power, and pretensions. Neither the ridicule of the skeptic nor the unbelief of the Christian will repress them. The true will begin to appear as well as the false. As the Church descends, as a new life buds up in the heart of the world, open visions will become more and more frequent, pregnant with truth and use and beauty. Swedenborg has given us the key whereby we may test all the spirits as the Apostle commanded. It is our duty to use it. We shall thereby warn men of the dangers which are springing upon them from the spiritual world; and be ready also to welcome the "glad tidings" which angelic messengers will certainly bring us from the same source.

The test or touchstone of good or evil spirits is plain and practical. There are two great central truths in the spiritual universe. No angel or good spirit is ignorant of them. Whatever doubts some good men may have had respecting them here, they are all dissipated by a little instruction in the world of spirits. These great truths are the following:

The Lord Jesus Christ in his Glorified Human Person is the Supreme God of the universe.

The Holy Scriptures are divine truth, having spiritual and celestial senses, meaning within meaning, adapted to men, spirits, and angels, according to their degree of life.

Faith in these doctrines, and a life according to the commandments given by the Lord through his Word, are the basis of heavenly character. A burning love for these doctrines creates a sphere of spiritual power in the minds of angels and good spirits, which protects them for ever from the assaults of evil ones. It is the same faith and love, the same sphere of the Lord and the Word, which works out our deliverance here from the bondage of sin, and leads us into the light and liberty of the Gospel. Evil spirits and devils hate these heavenly doctrines—hate the Divinity of Jesus Christ and the sanctity of the Word, and deny or ignore them in their communications with men.

When spirits profess to come from the Heavenly Country to reveal to us its beautiful laws and phenomena; to deliver us from the bondage of earthly error and darkness; and to lead us into the light and peace of eternal truth; and know nothing of the Lord and King of that Happy Land, confounding Him in his earth-life with Socrates, Seneca, and other teachers of morals; and when they seem ignorant of his Holy Word; of its illumining and sanctifying power over men, spirits, and angels; and of the boundless arcana of wisdom and beauty which are for ever being revealed in heaven from its inexhaustible fountains; how can we credit their utterances, or believe that they are any thing but wicked impostors?

Intercourse with angels being next to impossible on account of our hereditary and acquired evils; communication with spirits being dangerous and uncertain in the present condition of the race; the Lord has most mercifully prepared a great and good human medium, to whom He revealed the internal or spiritual sense of his Word, which harmonizes into a new and glorious unity of doctrine all the discrepancies of the letter, and who was permitted, under divine protection from assaulting falsities, to see and hear enough of the wonders behind the veil to illumine our minds, comfort our hearts, confirm our faith, and strengthen our love in a manner never before vouchsafed to mankind. The Coming Church will listen only to him, and to those who bring credentials similar to his own, stamped beyond question with the sign and seal of the Lord and the Word.

It is hard to give up all hope of a conscious communication with our departed treasures in the present life. Never to see their beautiful faces again; never to hear their sweet voices; never to press their little hands to our lips! Never! For in the weary length of despairing hours, this earth-life seems a forever to our grief. And yet it is better thus. We cannot precipitate ourselves into their states, nor cruelly draw them back into ours. The kindly influences which will bring us sweetly together are all at work; unseen but sure; softer than the dew, purer than the light, stronger than the electric girdle that binds the earth. Therefore let our souls "wait patiently on the Lord."

It is pleasant, however, very pleasant, to know that this seemingly utter separation is not an arbitrary decree of God—not a necessary condition of things; but a positive evil brought about by sin, continued upon our race by its own blindness and disobedience; an evil against which Providence continually contends for us, and which He will finally overcome for us, by means of his opening Word and ever-increasing angelic ministrations.

In the far future, which inevitably awaits mankind, when the moral world shall have described its destined orbit and the golden age returned again; when the light of the moon shall be as the light of the sun, and the light of the sun shall be sevenfold; we verily believe that in every household of the human race will be set up a Jacob's ladder—not in vision, but in reality—whereby will be restored for ever the lost communication between angels and men.

Our departed friends, however, very frequently communicate with our spirits in a manner which does not come within the range of our consciousness. We live, move, and think, in total ignorance or oblivion of by far the greater part of our own spiritual activities. We know no more of the secret operations of our interior life, than we do of the organic wonders going on in the anatomical recesses of our own bodies. These things will come to us after death like old and sweet memories. We will find many a familiar face about us, of whom we now know nothing. We will remember many happy visits, many kind and gentle services from those we call dead, and of which, in our earth-life, we had no perception. In that happy by-and-by, when all that is amiss in this world shall be readjusted, we shall discover the key to many a perplexity, the interpretation of many a dream.

It is a doctrine of Swedenborg that life, with all its affections and thoughts, flows downward from the Lord through the different heavens, and from them through the world of spirits into men; one and the same in its essence, infinitely varied in its manifestations according to the forms through which it flows; thus holding all parts of the universe in orderly connection, the entire unity being visible to the Lord alone. Man originates nothing, has nothing, is nothing of himself. He could not breathe or think or feel, unless he were adjoined to spirits, and through them to angels, who passed down the golden cup of life from one to another receiving it from the Lord, and pouring out the dregs upon the animals, the plants, and the minerals of the earth.

Nothing of this appears from an outside standpoint; and men have built up a vast sensuous philosophy of mind and matter, which discredits the spiritual theory altogether. When grounded and confirmed in their self-reliant materialism, which is based on the uncorrected evidence of their senses, it is almost as impossible for them, boasting of their riches of science and reason, to believe and be saved by a system of spiritual doctrine, as for a camel to go through the eye of a needle.

Every man seems to himself to occupy the central point in the universe, and the entire heavens actually communicate with the interiors of every human soul. When the outer senses are laid into a certain sleep, the interior faculties, communicating as they do with the spiritual world, may be awakened into astonishing activity. A man may see, hear, feel, and think, far more keenly when he seems asleep or dead to the natural eye, than he can when wide awake. He may become clairvoyant in that state, and see through all intervening obstacles. He may be filled with ideas and conceptions, which are evidently not his own. He may discourse fluently and learnedly on the most abstruse subjects, even in languages with which, when not asleep, he is totally unacquainted. He may dictate philosophical lectures or epic poems at a single sitting, and not be able to write a similar line of either when awake. When roused from his brief trance, he remembers nothing of what he has said or seen. The curtain falls upon his inner life, and he seems to live only in nature.

These things, and a thousand others of the same sort, verified over and over, illustrate some of the laws of that spiritual life into which we all awaken from the short and pleasant sleep of death. They are totally unsolvable by the materialistic philosophy, and are regarded as chimeras or hallucinations by those who cannot explain the facts in accordance with their favorite theories. They confirm the psychological doctrines of Swedenborg, and receive from them at the same time their best explanation.

It is in this world within our world; this spiritual Valley of Rasselas, walled in by great mountains from our common perceptions; this fairy-land of the soul, invisible to our mortal eyes; it is here that spirit meets spirit; it is here that the ministrations of angels and good spirits take place, and the mystical process of regeneration occurs. No sweet Egeria of that spiritual sphere may become visible in our dim grottoes, and impart to us that knowledge which is immortal food. The secret communings of our ethereal friends may be recognized by us only in the shape of whispers or dreams, or in the still more subtile forms of a renewed hope, a nourished faith, a happier resignation, or a brighter joy!

It is unquestionable that different orders and classes of glorious beings accompany us in all our changes of state or place. Some are the guardians of our sleep, and some of our labors. Some assist in our devotions, and others give zest to our innocent pleasures. They partake something also of our joys and our sorrows. They wait on all alike; on the savage and the sage; on the child bounding forth from their celestial sphere, and on the old man tottering back to their embrace. They sense our evil thoughts, and withdraw as at the hiss of serpents. They perceive our humility and our prayers, and they advance, attracted by a perfume as of violets and roses.

"Little infants are sometimes sent from heaven," says Swedenborg, "to little infants upon earth, who are affected thereby with ecstatic delight." What pearl of more exquisite beauty than that thought ever dropped from the singing lips of poet on earth! Perhaps our little ones also, when they look so brightly into the air, and leap with such strange gladness in our arms, behold little babes more beautiful than themselves, kissing them recognition through haloes of golden light.

Our spirit-friends frequently come to us with warning, advising, or encouraging dreams.

Dreams, so vague, so fantastic, so volatile! what are they but shifting scenes in the kaleidoscope of memory, *ignes fatui* of thought floating up from the senseless and sleeping body? Who knows or believes anything of the symbolic wisdom they may contain? That symbolic wisdom is so utterly lost to mankind, that the silly dream-books of the fortune-teller are all that remain of its glory, like some broken and tarnished marble from a temple of Persepolis.

Dreams are generally so senseless or incredible, that the word dreamer is a term of reproach. And yet all the poets and prophets of the world have been dreamers. The advanced and pivotal men of all ages and countries have delivered their utterances in a state of high trance to the uncomprehending multitudes. In this sense Swedenborg was the prince of dreamers. And although the dreamer of one age is the oracle of the next, the same thing perpetually occurs. The sensual-minded brethren of every new Joseph, when they see him afar off, exclaim to each other: "Behold! this dreamer cometh."

The dream-world is a picture-world, built up according to the same laws of correspondence which govern the real worlds surrounding men and spirits. The law of symbolism is universal. The external always represents some unseen internal. Angels in one heaven can watch the beautiful clouds in their sky, ever shifting in form and color, and read in their changes the variations of thought and affection of the angels in the heaven above them. This fact, transmitted to posterity and lost or perverted in its meaning, was the basis of ancient augury, which was a means of predicting the future from the flight of birds, the movements of clouds and winds, and other external phenomena.

This repetition, under symbolic images in a lower sphere and by different forms, of what is transacting in a higher, is as true of our world as of any other. Every object in nature has something spiritual concealed within it; every flower has some thought of ethereal beauty as the cause of its existence. This great truth, patent to all in the spiritual spheres, and to the inhabitants of sinless worlds, has been lost to our common perception, and is discovered only by the poetic faculty. The "sermons in stones" and the "books in the running brooks," are not imaginary but real. The sounding cataract, which haunts the poet "like a passion," and the little violet, half concealing its modest face behind mossy stones, have living, spiritual voices within them, which have reached the poet's ear and touched his open heart with wonder and joy.

The dreams recorded in the Bible illustrate the symbolic character of dreams generally, being always representative of interior and spiritual things. Swedenborg says that the men of the golden age were visited by the most charming dreams from heaven, by which they were not only delighted, but greatly instructed, because they perceived intuitively the meaning involved in the minutest circumstance of the visions. In later ages they not only lost the secret key to their dreams, but by the increasing influx of evil spirits they began to have false, evil, and fantastic dreams. Finally, when the interiors were closed, and man became merely sensual, the dream degenerated into the present confused and unintelligible thing, a mere cobweb, in which fancy and memory are buzzing like entangled flies.

In the restoration of all things, when the aggregate human mind is reduced to states of perfect order and beauty, the dream will recover its old power and significance as a most beautiful and charming mode of communication between the higher and lower spheres of existence. One of the blessings promised to the crowned and perfected Church is, that "the old men shall dream dreams, and the young men shall see visions."

Swedenborg describes clearly and from frequent experience the manner in which the conversation of angels or spirits, who are present with a man in sleep, are turned into dreams of persons, things, or events, perfectly representative of the subject of discourse. Sometimes the simplest, most trivial dreams are the outward expressions of wonderful spiritual communications. Our external memory treasures the mere dream; our internal or spiritual memory stores away its spiritual significance. Our best dreams, those productive of the profoundest influence on our souls, may not come so far forth into the external memory as to be remembered in our waking state.

We adduce, as an example of the warning dream,

one which occurred to a New Churchman, who had been plunged into a state of dreadful darkness and despair by the loss of two beautiful children. He of course understood the correspondences contained in the vision; and it haunted him like a living presence until he was delivered by Divine Providence from his temptations. It is given in his own words:

"I saw in my dream a tall, black, hairy man, with features like an ape, ascending from a dark place which seemed very full of rocks. He carried a great knotted staff in his hand, longer than himself, reaching above his head. This strange figure looked eagerly around as if searching for some one. His physiognomy, exceedingly repulsive, was now somewhat softened by an air of anxious curiosity, almost of tenderness. He expected to meet his little children. Death had torn them from him, and left him bleeding and stumbling in this dark world of sin. Now he also was a spirit. The good Lord had permitted these near akin but separated souls, 'so near and yet so far,' to greet each other once more. The poor father will see his dear little children—his jewels—his idols—again! What happiness!

"Very soon, descending from a luminous circle

in the east, came forward along a green slope two children hand-in-hand, a little boy and a little girl. Radiant as angels, beautiful as dreams, they floated rather than walked over the ground. They peered with bright loving eyes and eager shining faces into the dusky atmosphere which surrounded the strange man. Their little hearts palpitated with joy. They were about to meet their 'papa,' whom they had left weeping over their little dying bodies —dying in the same week! In their tender imaginations their 'dear papa' was so young, so handsome, such a glorious Apollo! Ah, my God! What children! What a father!

"The parties, so anxiously anticipating this meeting, approach. They see each other and stop. The dark, hairy man, an ape in the light of heaven, letting fall his rough staff, throws his hands up into the air, exclaiming with wild delight: 'My children! My children!' The little ones survey him with pale faces and stupefied air. They cling more closely to each other; they tremble; they cry out in one breath: 'It is not my papa! No—no—no! It is not my papa!' They turn away; they fly with trepidation up the green slope. One sweet little voice, half weeping, dies away in the distance: 'Not my papa!'

"The wretched father, wildly excited, pursues them. 'Come back, my children! It is I! It is I, your own papa! Oh, come back, my children!' The dark rocks on either hand respond in mockery: 'My children!' Suddenly the little creatures, very much affrighted, turn into two beautiful white Doves. They fly with swift-beating wings towards the auroral windows of the east. The miserable father stops astonished. He gazes after them, bent eagerly forward. What an attitude! what a face! He watches them intently, until they become two little silver specks fading into the background of golden light. Then all darkens around him, and he raises a great shriek of agony: 'They are Angels; they are Angels: and I am a Lost Spirit!'

"The earth yawned, and the strange man fell into the pit, the dark rocks tumbling after him.

"I awoke, cold, suffocated, trembling, weeping.

"I had reason. The Lost Spirit was myself!"

There are two still more subtile and powerful means of secret communication with our lost friends, unknown to men or discredited by them because they are not recognized by our external consciousness. The first is effected by the Word of God when it is read simultaneously by the two parties, the one on earth understanding it literally it may be, the other in heaven understanding it in a spiritual manner. The second means is a closer unition of our interior souls by similar progressions in the great work of regeneration.

The Holy Bible is a wonderful link or bond of union between human thought and angelic thought, and so between heaven and earth. It exists in both worlds, and is far more constantly, reverently, and fruitfully studied by angels than by men. In that heavenly Bible there is not one word of Abraham or Isaac or Jacob, of David or John, of Egypt or Canaan, or of any historical event that has ever occurred; but in their places the spiritual truths of the Lord's Kingdom, which those names and occurrences represented.

When a person upon earth reads the Bible in a prayerful and reverential spirit, the angels come very much nearer to him, because they are drawn or attracted by the beautiful spiritual truths which are contained in the letter. This is the secret of the vast influence of the Bible upon the world and upon the individual heart of man. When angelic thought is thus brought into rapport with human thought, angelic affections excite or arouse into activity the little germs of similar affections existing in man. In all this the Lord works unseen, Himself the Source of all life and love. Hence the noble virtues and charming graces of the Christian character! Hence the faith that survives criticism and defies extinction! Hence the love which outgrows its earthly bonds, and is liberated at death for measureless expansion!

Yes, dear Parent! believe it. When you sit in your quiet chamber, the scene perhaps of so much suffering and sorrow, and in the soft light of a Sabbath evening read the sweet stories of Moses and Joseph and Samuel, or the wonderful history of the birth and childhood of Jesus; when you awake the soft minor strains of the Psalmist, or the solemn organ-tones of the Prophets, or the mighty voices and thunderings of the Apocalypse; your Little Ones will come very near to you, like invisible doves hovering about your shoulders with olive-branches in their mouths. A subtile power will pass from them into your own soul; and if you could see the new life, the new love, the new faith imparted, as you will one day feel them, you would exclaim with Jacob awaking from his dream: "This is none other but the house of God, and this is the gate of heaven."

The best and surest method of communication,

for it leads to eternal union, is to grow more and more like our children. Similarity of character is the bond of association in the life to come. Your nearest neighbors there are those most like yourself. All the members of each angelic society think alike and feel alike, with none but harmonic differences. They are conjoined together by secret spiritual affinities on the principle of use, like the various organs, tissues, and minutest cells of the human body.

While living here upon earth, our spirits are really traveling from society to society in the spiritual world. The man who was avaricious once, but is generous now; the man who has passed from intemperate to abstinent habits; the man who has put the demon of licentiousness under his feet; all have changed their locations in the spiritual world, so that the spirits who knew them once, now know them no more. We do not see these spiritual routes we are taking, for the Lord's providence leads us by ways unknown; but they are as real as any earthly journeys by land or water.

We are traveling every day to or from our beloved ones. Spirits of the same family and blood are specially drawn to each other by secret ties and attractions, and the good of many generations are frequently collected together in sweet companionship and in the same heavenly society. It is the Lord's good will that we shall rejoin our dear ones, and his loving-kindness is ever striving to lead us together. For this purpose He would keep ever before our spiritual eyes the little wicket gate, shining like a star, which leads through the Valley of Humiliation to the green pastures and placid waters of the happy country of the Good Shepherd.

Our departed friends are undergoing a continual process of purification. They are becoming more and more heavenly, less and less earthly. They are casting off for ever the lusts and errors of this world, the pride and selfishness, even the petulance, the obstinacy, the conceitedness, the little imperfections of our characters. They are moving toward the great and beautiful ideals of angelic life. They are being transfigured in every feature and gesture by spiritual processes, and their faces are beginning to shine like that of Moses when he conversed with God on Sinai.

Bereaved and sorrowing ones! is it so with us? Are we dropping the old states of our sensual life, as a tree sheds its leaves? Are we conscious of a steady spiritual transformation within ourselves?

Are we following the track of those over whom we wept so bitterly? Do we keep them ever in sight? Or are we living in sensual pleasures, with no high and holy aspirations, but turning continually to self and the world? If so, we are becoming more and more unlike those we loved so tenderly. A chasm is yawning between us, dark and deep; a chasm of spiritual repulsions and antipathies, which will widen and widen until it becomes the Impassable Gulf.

Awful thoughts! That we may become so evil that we will never see our children again! That they may become so pure, that no memories of us shall ever visit their happy spirits, "coming, like ghosts, to trouble joy!" That the few years of earth-life, when parent and child were bound heart to heart—the few years so happy, so loved, so wept, may sink into eternal oblivion and be lost, like a pearl fallen to the bottom of the sea!

CHAPTER VIII.

WHY DID NOT THE LORD PREVENT?

MANY years ago, when a terrible epidemic was desolating the city of New Orleans, a poor fellow who had led a reckless, irreligious life, was about giving it up to the great destroyer. All hope was gone: his physician had retired. An old nurse and a solitary friend, wearied with night-watching, were dozing at the bed-side, waiting for the patient to breathe his last. The sick man, although retaining his senses, lay in that torpid and indifferent state which sometimes precedes death.

A kind-hearted clergyman on his morning round of benevolent visitation, stepped into the room, startling the sleepers into watchfulness again. He knew the circumstances and character of the dying man, and addressed him immediately to the point.

"My dear friend," he said, "you have lived a wicked and sinful life, and are now about to appear, unprepared I am afraid, before the Judge of the whole earth. I feel warranted, however, in making to you, in the name of our Saviour, a last appeal. He who heard the prayer of the penitent thief, is ready to answer yours also, if you make it in the proper spirit."

The sick man slowly turned his bronzed face and bloodshot eyes on the speaker, but said nothing.

The preacher continued:

"You have but little time left for preparation. Do not waste it on idle memories of the past or useless speculations about the future. Address yourself earnestly to the throne of grace. The divine sympathy may yet be aroused in your behalf. Let me pray for you and with you!"

There was no answer.

"Are you not afraid to meet your God," said the clergyman, with a little determination in his tone.

"Oh no!" muttered the dying man, very slowly but with some emphasis, "not at all afraid to meet my God."

"On what, pray, sir! do you base your hope of salvation? Your answer, permit me to say, smacks of irreverent presumption. Remember that you have been a man without God and without religion in this world. What is there to support you in the hour of death?"

"I have had a religion, and a very good one," muttered the other, as if talking to himself.

Then suddenly starting up on his elbow, he exclaimed with surprising energy and intelligence:

"Listen, sir! I thank you for your kind feelings and your good intentions; but really I need none of your offices. Many years ago, when I was a little boy, I attended a Sunday-school in my native village in the State of New York."

He paused and gazed into vacancy, half-smiling, as if some sweet memories had suddenly broken in upon him. The clergyman moved a step nearer to him, and he continued:

"Behind the leader's desk was a golden sun painted upon the wall, with these words in its centre:

"'God is Love.'

That picture sank into my boy's heart, and I have seen it ever since.—I see it now.—That is my religion.—That is my God."

He sank exhausted on his pillow. The kind minister forebore to press his gospel invitation, and looked on in pitying silence

The dying man bent his head far back, looking directly upwards, and muttered faintly as if still answering the clergyman's question:

"Oh no! sir. I may be afraid of man, but I am not, cannot be, afraid of God."

The speaker was expiring.

The minister lifted his eyes deprecatingly and turned away. He heard the death-rattle ere he reached the door. If his spiritual eyes had been opened at that moment, he would have seen shining visitors crowding about the dying sinner.

What visitors?

The angels of the resurrection!

This little anecdote is given, not to encourage any false hopes of a happy future after an evil life, but as a forcible expression of the great central truth of religion, that the Lord is a being of infinite and perfect love and mercy. The law of the Divine Love is the "higher law" of the spiritual universe—yea, the Highest Law, which overrules and determines all others. It is the all-pervading element of a pure faith, and must dominate the intellect without any qualifying clause. Every seeming law or statement which is inconsistent with a perfect conception of the law of Divine Love, is either false in itself, or is some truth perverted and corrupted in its passage through the disorderly or incapable mind of man.

A piece of ice seems to our senses utterly destitute of heat. It has other properties and exhibits the operation of other laws, mechanical, chemical, optical, and electrical. Still the law of Heat is the fundamental law of its existence and form. Modify its relation to Heat, and all its phenomena—as light, shape, color, cohesion, chemical and electrical powers—are so changed that its identity cannot be recognized. So the Divine Love is the essential life of the universe, and its reception by created forms determines the spiritual and natural qualities they manifest. There is no object or person or place or state in which this supreme law, God is Love, does not reign over all things, in spite of appearances to the contrary.

We will take this little text with us from the walls of the village Sunday-school, and it shall be our guiding star through all imaginable darknesses and perplexities. When men deny God, or accuse Him falsely, because there is disorder and sickness in the world, and horrible crimes and sufferings, and ages of barbarism and slavery; we answer in the face of all this evil—God is Love. He caused none of it and is responsible for none of it. He resists it continually; He never, never permits it when He can prevent it; He educes good from it always; and He will subdue it eventually.

When we look into the Holy Scriptures and see that God is said to tempt men to acts of disobedience; to harden their hearts and then destroy them; to do great works and then repent of having done them; to be wrathful against his enemies; to command one nation to exterminate another; to give us blessings and then take them away; to laugh at our calamities and to mock at our fear; we see by the sweet light of our golden text, that these are fallacies, the mere sensuous appearances of the letter uncorrected by the light of spiritual interpretation. We know in our inmost hearts that God never changes, never tempts, is never angry, never punishes, never gives and then takes away.

We may penetrate even into hell and see myriads of evil spirits living in states far lower, more bestial and painful than our saddest types of Indian or African or Australian barbarism. We may discover in that doleful region wickedness and its attendant suffering, in comparison with which all our crimes and sorrows are but the seed in proportion to the harvest; and still our motto, God is

Love, shines as sweetly and softly in those lurid atmospheres as in the azure skies of heaven. The Love of God is there also, not to punish or destroy, but to maintain order, to protect, to sustain, to alleviate, to amend, and, so far as may be possible, to reclaim.

God creates man, not for his glory and a display of his power, but from his boundless love, yearning to give Himself away, as it were, in innumerable forms of life and beauty, to an ever-increasing multitude which no man can number, of good, wise, and happy beings capable of receiving and reciprocating that love. Behold there a motive worthy of a God! His will is, that all should be good and wise and happy and perfect in their spheres. His will is, that blessings and riches and honors should be showered upon every head; and that every path should be strewn with flowers from the cradle to the grave. His will is, that there should be no pain or sickness, and no removal from earth until man attains the ripeness and fullness of natural life, that serene old age of this world which hardly conceals the radiant youthfulness of the next. His will is, to flood every human heart with the fullest tides of love, peace, beauty, and joy!

"Thy kingdom come. Thy will be done on Earth as it is in Heaven!"

Whenever and wherever these things are not found, but their opposites appear—evil, falsity, poverty, pain, crime, and early death; we may rest perfectly assured that the will of God has not been done. Some Evil One hath sown tares among the wheat. Some discord has crept into the music of the spheres. Who has thwarted the will of the Omnipotent. The questions, how?—when?—wherefore? crowd upon us. We are oppressed with a sense of mystery. Doubts and despairs like clouds spread over the whole heaven. The Universe becomes a riddle; the Word of God a closed Book, sealed with seven seals; and like the beloved Apostle, the bewildered Christian "weeps much, that no man can break the seals and open the Book and read therein."

One of the Elders before the throne said to John:

"Weep not! Behold! the Lion of the Tribe of Judah, the Root of David, hath prevailed to open the Book and to loose the seven seals thereof."

What the Apostle saw in vision is now passing into history. This opening of the Book, celebrated by the glorifications of angels to the number of "ten thousand times ten thousand and thousands of thousands," is the same event as the Second Coming of the Lord, not bodily in the clouds of heaven, but with spiritual and angelic light and glory into the dark clouds of the Letter of the Word. This Revelation of the Spiritual Sense of the Holy Scripture has been made in these latter days through an Illuminated Medium; and it contains a new philosophy, a new psychology, a new theology, for the use of a New Church, the New Jerusalem; in which heaven and earth—"the new heaven and the new earth"—shall be once more and for ever united.

He has come as He predicted, "like a thief in the night;" and has found but little faith on the earth. He walks along the wayside with those who love Him best and seek Him most, explaining from Moses and the Prophets what was written of Himself; but their eyes are holden and they do not know Him.

The Doctrine of the Lord which the Spiritual Sense teaches, is the true doctrine, rising above the appearances of the Letter, and the mist and fallacies of merely natural thought. Philosophy or Religion without a true knowledge of God, is a body without a heart, a nation without a head, a world without a sun. Our conception of God is the eye through which we see everything.

"If therefore thine eye be single, thy whole body shall be full of light. But if thine eye be evil, thy whole body shall be full of darkness."

What, then, is the conception of God, from which, as from a very high spiritual mountain, we may look down into the causes of things, see the origin and uses of evil, and why the Lord does not prevent it?

The Lord Jesus Christ, in his risen and glorified Human Form, is the Supreme Being—the Only God—one in essence and in person. Out of Him there is no Father and no Holy Ghost. What these terms express are mere abstractions apart from the person of Jesus Christ; they are hindrances not helps to a true knowledge and worship of Him. This Lord, the God-Man, in whom "dwelleth all the fullness of the Godhead bodily," is the uncreated source of all Life and Goodness. No life or goodness we may discover in man is ever self-originated, but always derived from the same central Fountain. "There is none good but God."

This Divine Goodness flows down and presses in and pours outward in living streams, causing all the life, goodness, peace, joy, wisdom, beauty, and excellence in the world. It strives to communicate itself to all alike, to the evil and the good; to create a heaven in every human heart, thereby predestinating and willing every human being to have a place in heaven. It possesses also infinite Wisdom to conceive and plan, and infinite Power to execute what it so ardently desires. Surely His will shall finally be done on earth as it is in heaven!

This original, holy, beatific, super-excellent Ideal of a creation, full of good and wise beings, preparing on happy worlds for happier heavens, has been broken and would have been destroyed, at least on this earth, but for His own Incarnation. His Divine Mind and Will, however, have not changed. He still strives to carry out his original plan and to realize His divine ideal of universal felicity and salvation. His providence labors incessantly to bring the world and every individual back to the state of divine order contemplated from the beginning. No change in His finite creatures can ever effect any change in Himself. He has no anger; no impatience; no accusing spirit; no avenging justice; no finite qualifications to his infinite and unchangeable love and pity. He gives, gives, gives; and He never takes away anything good or true or beautiful, without providing something better, truer, and more beautiful. Such is the Lord as He really is behind the clouds of sensuous perception, which like the Letter of the Word conceal for a while His true nature and glory from us.

The rainbow-colors are as beautiful in the dew-drop as in the vaulted sky. Universal Truths are seen alike in the greatest things and in the least; in the extinction of a sun and in the falling of a sparrow. This great truth of the Divine Love must come home to every human heart, and to the little circumstances of our daily lives.

Ah! poor, bereaved, Christian mother! who knelt so humbly at His feet, and wept so bitterly and prayed so fervently that your precious child—your heart's wealth—might be spared to you; and all in vain, in vain! You cannot see the Divine Love in the sun-colors in which our philosophy has painted it. In your great affliction it seemed to you that the Lord was far, far away; forgetful and unmindful of your sorrows; delaying to come, as he did to Lazarus; or when He came, shorn of His miraculous power.

Perhaps your stricken soul, bewildered by a terrible theology, imagined even that He, in His austere wisdom—knowing what, though cruel, was best—summoned from their awful deeps the blood-hounds of darkness, and set them upon the track of your innocent and helpless one. Your only comfort is the belief, that in some inscrutable manner all this misery was necessary and proper for your final salvation and the child's. In the sweet but despairing resignation of your faith, you struggle to exclaim—"Thy will de done!"

Now ascend that Spiritual mountain with Peter and James and John, on which our Lord can always be seen in another form and in a holier light. In your sad bereavement, every cruel incident of which you so vividly remember, the Lord was present, resisting every step of the process by which your little one was torn from you. He descended through spiritual atmospheres and through good spirits and angels into your very chamber. So far as He could, consistently with universal laws, and according to the spiritual forms into which He was obliged to flow, He inspired your physicians with wisdom, your nurses with watchfulness, your remedies with healing virtues, and the very elements around you with conspiring influences in your behalf. Better question his Omnipotence than doubt His Love.

We seldom realize the intensely personal relation which God endeavors to establish with our hearts. To the intellect He is the supreme Intelligence, creating and sustaining the Universe; to the heart, He is the sympathizing Friend, Father, Saviour. We know Him in His great kingdom without; we can love Him only in His little kingdom within us. It is His boundless love for our children, which we receive in our finite spirits, and feel as if it were entirely our own. Our anxieties, our temptations, our hopes, our aspirations are His also. He enters into and clothes Himself with our spiritual infirmities as He once did with a material body. He is near us in our dark hours, and nearest in the darkest. He contends with the Powers of Darkness for the life of every little child, like Michael contending with the devil for the body of Moses: and He stands in tears at every little grave, as He stood with Mary and Martha at the grave of Lazarus.

If all this be true, why do our children die? If God is a Being of infinite Love, Wisdom and Power, why does He permit evil to invade His dominion, to thwart His will, to defeat His plans, to disorganize His world, to torture and destroy His creatures, and to endanger the peace and even the existence of His heavens? Why did He not ordain it otherwise? Why slumbers His justice? Where is the proof of His Omnipotence?

Before attempting to throw some new light on these old questions, so full of primeval darkness and difficulty, it will be necessary to show why the literal sense of the Bible militates against our view of the Divine Love and Providence—for the Word of God is our sole guide in doctrinal matters. Why is God there described as a jealous God, a Being of inexorable justice, who is angry with the sinner every day, and who dooms the unrepentant to an eternal hell? Why is He said to chasten those He loves, to afflict them for their good, to give and to take away from them at his unexplained pleasure, and to purify them as by fire? These ideas are so plainly inculcated in the letter, and are so thoroughly interwoven into the doctrines and life of the Christian Church, that men cling to them with intense affection and feel that to give them up, is to give up the Bible, the Church, and even the Lord Himself. And yet it is not so. There is a better way, a purer light. The Bible has a Soul also which lives in the midst of its body.

Every jot and tittle of the Holy Scripture exists

in heaven; and yet not one word of the letter, as we read it, can enter there. We leave the literal sense behind us at death, just as we leave our natural bodies; and we enter into possession of the spiritual sense. That spiritual sense has now been opened for us by the Lord, and we can discover the jewels of spiritual truth which were concealed in so plain a casket. This is the origin of the new light which enables us to correct our view of the Divine nature.

The Bible was communicated from heaven in a sense and by a method quite unknown to the Christian Church. It was not a simple dictation from the Lord or angels to chosen men, or the inspired word of worthy mediums filled with the Divine Spirit. It is from that stand-point the infidel assails it so successfully, subjecting the terrible difficulties of the letter to his pitiless criticism, and mocking at its divinity. The Word exists in heaven as a glorious coherent body of spiritual truth; the direct, thought-giving effluence of the Divine Mind. In passing through the minds of the medium—for it descended by an internal way—it took on a human vestment from their natural thought, limited by time, place, and circumstance; and issued forth a very different thing in appearance from what it was and still is in its heavenly interiors.

When an angel speaks to man, he seems to speak in the man's native tongue, whatever that may be. The angel does not know nor can he utter a word of human language. His spiritual ideas, passing through the interiors of the man's mind, take on a clothing or investment from the man's natural memory of words before they are presented to his own consciousness. So the Divine Word has clothed itself in the ideas and words of the Jewish mind. It would have had very different histories, prophecies, poems, all with precisely the same spiritual sense, if some other nation had been selected for a representative church. Passing through the Greek mind, it would have assumed probably a far more artistic and philosophical shape. The Jews were chosen, so that the Word might descend in accommodating forms to the lowest and most sensuous phase of human life and thought. Those who touch "even the hem of His garment" are saved.

Spiritual truths flowing through a human mind derive an external shape or form from the peculiarities of the mental structure. The extreme degree of deviation or perversion occurs when a spiritual truth is let down into the mind of a demon, one who has been divested of all goodness and is thoroughly evil. The idea is then turned into its exact opposite. This experiment was repeated several times for Swedenborg's instruction. All falsities are thus the perversions of truths passing through disordered minds. A perfect, symmetrical Revelation can only be made through angelic minds, whose minutest fibres are in musical accord with the breath of heaven. No spiritual truth can be transmitted through human mediums, without losing something of its clearness, power, and beauty. This psychological law is one of the keys to Biblical interpretation.

Our ideas of God depend entirely on the degree of spiritual light into which we can be elevated. In one state we see Him as a powerful Being, jealous of His glory, rewarding His friends, punishing His enemies, and demanding an eye for an eye and a tooth for a tooth. In another state we see Him as a divided Being, His justice appearing to us under one form, His mercy under another, and His ministering power under a third. In a still more advanced stage of development, He appears to us as a Divine Man, governing with infinite wisdom and mercy all things alike in heaven, earth, and hell. What seems to be a truth from one stand-point, becomes a falsity from another.

One man sees God in a little image of wood or stone—amazing narrowness and darkness of thought! Even that conception serves to keep alive in his heart the feeble germs of faith and veneration, and is better than no idea at all. Another, without approaching a step nearer to Him, sees Him in the glorious mechanism of the Universe, which, abstracted from the personal Spirit of God, is only a large idol or fetich. Many of us know Him only as a mysterious Power wrestling with our souls, as the angel is said to have wrestled with Jacob in the dark. Blind and unhappy is the man who can look around and within and not see Him at all!

In the race as in the individual, the first stage of mental life is sensuous. It is the age of miracles and not of reason. It is only the preparation of the ground for future growth. Man then lives in various fallacies of thought derived from sensuous appearances, from which he cannot be extricated but as the chick is extricated from the shell—by a process of development. For him the sun moves round the world; ceremonies are the essentials of the Church; and God punishes His enemies and rewards His friends with the animus of an earthly monarch. Such was the Jewish Church; and such are all those at this day who demand miracles as evidences of truth.

The race and the church as well as the individual advance next to a rational or metaphysical stage, retaining a great deal of their sensuous faith, but endeavoring to explain and justify it by doctrinal dogmas. The great difficulty with this phase of thought is, to reconcile the spiritual elements of the Old Theology with the rational principles of the New Science continually blossoming into view. The history of opinion here proves that the unillumined reason is as poor a guide to truth as the uninstructed senses. Such was the Apostolic Church, and such are now its thousand fragments.

In the manhood of the race, of the church, and of the individual, the critical spirit works incessantly to free itself from all errors, all theories, all masters; and to get at the positive light of truth. This positive stage of thought has two forms, only one of which was foreseen by the subtile author of the Positive Philosophy. One school gets rid of all our sensuous fallacies, including the religious intuitions, and of all our transitional metaphysics; bases itself on pure science; and, as might have been expected, lives in nature only, like a sagacious beast. The Swedenborgian School extricates itself entirely from the past, accepts a new Revelation from heaven, and makes all things freshly and eternally positive by viewing man, nature, science, history, and the Written Word in its spiritual light. The Positive Scientific School is a mere servant or vanguard, preparing the way by its critical and destructive energies for the universal domination of the Spiritual Philosophy.

Thus we see that it was organically impossible for the earlier ages and churches to have had correct ideas of the nature of God. There was a series of false doctrines (called by Swedenborg *apparent* truths, because they appeared true from the stand-point of the believers, and were accepted by the Lord as if they were true) permitted to men, just as polygamy was permitted to the Jews on account of "the hardness of their hearts." Every sin, it has been said, is the round of a ladder, which, if trodden under foot, leads us upward to the skies. So these false conceptions and erroneous opinions of the Church of God were not to be lived in, but lived out and left behind. Thus only can we advance nearer and nearer to the supernal light of genuine or spiritual truth.

Unless the Jews had been permitted to entertain the most external and sensuous ideas of God and his government, they would have had no idea at all; and a literal Word, bearing its true meaning concealed in its bosom, could not have been revealed to them. Unless man had been permitted to believe in a terrible hell and a sensuous heaven, he could never have been imbued with a spiritual aspiration. Unless he had been permitted to believe in the resurrection of the material body, he would have retained no faith in the immortality of the soul. Unless he had been permitted to see God in a three-fold form, as Father, Son, and Holy Spirit, no conception of the divinity of Jesus Christ could have been generated in his mind. Unless he had been permitted to attribute his sufferings and sorrows in some way to the Divine Providence, his faith would have staggered and his love perished in his great spiritual struggles.

How can the existence and continuance of Evil be reconciled with this last, loftiest, and purest conception of the Divine Character?

If human life was a power or force created by God and infused into an objective universe of forms called forth from nothing; if the creation was an external act of His, as a machine is the work of a man—and such is the popular belief; then indeed we would have great reason to find fault with the result, and to impeach the power, goodness, wisdom, and foreknowledge of the Creator. A universe created by Infinite Intelligence out of his own materials and on his own plan, has worked so sadly out of order in so short a time, that, viewing the subject from that stand-point, we certainly could not call it a complete success. We should call it, upon the whole, a failure.

But that view of life and of creation is radically false. Life is uncreated. God alone is Life. His Life is the only one that ever is, was, or shall be fluent in any organized form, human, animal, or vegetable. No other life is possible. He does not divide it and give one portion to this form and another portion to another. It is indivisible and always the same. Its myriad-fold manifestations depend only on the atomic arrangement of the forms into which it flows. It is not communicated to matter and then transmitted ever after from one thing to another. No: the whole vitality or life of the universe to-day flows into it from God to-day, from moment to moment; and if God could possibly cease living or breathing for a second, or if He should for one moment withhold His influent life from the countless forms He has created, the entire universe would dissolve into nothing. The act of creation is perpetual.

How then is Man, the central figure of the creation, "the image and likeness" of God? How is he different from God? If he is made of atomic substances proceeding from God, and animated entirely by life flowing in momentarily from God, is he not as much an integral part of the Divine Being as a man's fingers and toes are integral parts of his body? What can rescue us from Pantheism? How can man enjoy any sense of individuality, any feeling of identity, and a consciousness of himself?

Right here lies the first great secret of creation, the key to many of its enigmas. Unless man, in becoming finite, had acquired the power of reacting against God, that is, of receiving and using His influent life in one manner or another, just as he pleased, he would truly have had no sense of his individuality; no consciousness of his own mental operations; he would have been a mere automaton; an insensible, unreflective machine; and the object of the creation would never have been attained,—that object being not only the reception but the *reciprocation* of the Divine Love.

That reactive power is the free-will or free-agency of man.

The free-agency of man is therefore the ground or basis of his differentiation from God; of his seemingly independent vitality; of his progressive life to or from the Divine centre, and of his moral responsibility.

This fact is as broad, deep, original, and for the present almost as incomprehensible a necessity as the altogether inexplicable existence of God Himself. It is impossible for God not to create; it is simply the law or mode of His own life. It is equally impossible for Him to create a thinking, loving, reciprocating being, separated or discreted from Himself, except as a Free-Agent capable of reacting against the divine influx.

God, therefore, always preserves, protects, and respects the absolute free-agency of man, as the only ground of his rational and spiritual life. He governs him, draws him, leads him only by love, never by force or violence. Every angel in heaven and every devil in hell has gone to the exact place he now inhabits of his own free choice; and however miserable the surroundings of the latter may be, he cannot be persuaded to leave them. This extreme statement will show that man is permitted to do good or evil, to be good or evil, to remain good or evil, just as his own interior volitions may dictate. Man is, therefore, entirely responsible for all the violations of the divine law, and the consequent disorders and miseries which have created a hell and covered the world with its horrible shadow.

Whilst the potentiality or power to sin is woven into the structure of all beings in earth or heaven; the actuality, the fall from a state of order and purity into evil, has been, according to Swedenborg, of exceedingly limited extent. Myriads of myriads of beautiful worlds, the light of whose suns comes to us as that of little stars, or does not reach us at all, have been full for immeasurable ages of happy human beings, who have lived in voluntary obedience to the divine law. They have experienced none of the awful changes which have occurred through sin in other solar systems, and especially on our globe, the only one in the universe where it has been necessary for the Divine Being to incarnate himself as a Brother Man, to save men from the destruction they were bringing on themselves.

Evil thus originates in the power man has of turning away the interior forms of his spirit from God. When a spirit turns away from God and the neighbor to self and the world, listening to that old serpent, our sensual principle, an organic change takes place in the substance—in what we may call the atomic arrangement—of his spiritual brain; a change as real as the pathological changes in our tissues in cases of disease. The medium is then bent or distorted, so that the divine life flowing in from above is perverted in its passage through the changed form; and is manifested outwardly as something more or less evil and false instead of something good and true. The different properties of diamond and charcoal, both forms of carbon, illustrate finely what changes may be made in the same substance by a change in its atomic or molecular arrangement. So of the spirit.

God's life is the only life in heaven, earth and hell. In evil forms his love is turned into hatred, his truth into falsity, his light into darkness, his beauty into deformity, his peace into trouble, his felicity into woe. Thus the healthy and nutritious blood of man is changed into morbid secretions when it passes into some organ of the body which has been perverted from its normal type. Thus the heat and light of the sun, which are changed into the perfume and beauty of the flower, passing through some vegetable germ deflected from the lines of perfect order, produce some rank, ugly and poisonous object.

Evil men and evil spirits have moreover transcribed their interior perversions on the plastic face of nature; for all forces come from within outward, and produce their effects in the lowest or natural sphere of life. This is the origin of all the evil things we see around us; the poisons of the vegetable world; the cruel and hideous forms of animal life; the storms, the floods, the fires; the destructive extremes of heat and cold; the catastrophes which appall and overwhelm; the horrible diseases which waste our bodies; and the painful death that awaits our departure. All these things are outward effects, symbolic of the evil and false principles reigning in the hearts of men. God never causes them nor brings them nor sends them. Man alone is responsible for them. No such things exist in heaven, nor on any physical globe whose inhabitants have always kept the Divine commandments. All these things will disappear by a process the reverse of that by which they came. The dreams of the optimist will be fulfilled, because the entire means of their fulfillment lie in the enlightened volition of man himself.

When men became so averse to God and his

government that after death, they could not be inserted into angelic societies and made inhabitants of heaven, they were permitted to collect together, so that a different spiritual world could be created around them, as far from God and angels as possible, where they might live as they pleased; and that world is called Hell. It is a sphere of horrible hatreds, fantasies and sufferings, where all is evil, false and unreal. The inhabitants are there permitted to shroud themselves from the rays of Divine Love and Wisdom by dense atmospheres of evil and falsity, as the cuttle-fish hides himself from his enemy by ejecting a black fluid all around his form. This is of the divine mercy; for the divine presence is a torment to those miserable beings. "Art thou come hither to torment us?" is ever the sorrowful cry of lost spirits to the approaching Christ.

This idea, that hell is a world where the wicked continue the evil life they began here, and where the wail of the infinite divine pity mingles softly with the lamentations of the self-destroyed; this beautiful idea is offensive to the Christian mind which has been cast in the Israelitish mould. Such a mind believes that hell is a place of fearful punishment, which the divine justice inflicts eternally on the incorrigible. It believes that punishment is deserved; and that it is incompatible with the dignity and holiness of the Divine Being to permit his equitable laws to be violated with impunity.

This idea, full of the appearance of truth, is still far below the truth. There is darkness in it,—brought from the natural, civil and social spheres of our life,—which obscures the pure spiritual light. The spiritual idea is, that evil is organically its own punishment. The awful punishment of doing evil is that you become evil, so that you have no disposition to do otherwise. The punishment is in your own state and in the restraints which, for your own and others' good, Divine Love sees it to be necessary to impose upon your evil lusts. God does not inflict punishment. On the contrary, the boundless ingenuities of his providence are continually exercised to avert it, to modify it, to weaken its violence, and to deliver from it.

It is a terrible idea—but oh how true!—that sin perverts and corrupts the spiritual form, just as disease does the natural body. Look at the fearful ravages which intemperance and licentiousness make on the human face; the horrible diseases and sufferings which result from their domination; and the utter and pitiable bondage of the poor victims to their own sinful and cruel passions; and you have the whole story of sin and its punishment; of a hell begun in this world and continued in the next; of that awful Hall of Eblis, where the ghastly skeletons in silent frenzy wander about in their black cloaks, each concealing a burning heart under his ribs.

This self-inflicted punishment of sin, originating from interior causes, is very different from the punishments of an exterior nature sometimes inflicted by men and spirits on each other. An instinct of self-preservation authorizes us to defend ourselves against assaults upon what is peculiarly our own. Society and governments defend themselves also against assailants of their life or peace. Laws are made on this principle for the regulation of society, of the family, of the school, etc. Offenders are punished according to the nature and extent of the crime. These punishments are cruel and barbarous if dictated by hatred and vengeance. They may be very wise and humane if prevention and reform are the real ends in view. It is from this purely finite and external conception of human justice and self-defence, that man has devised the monstrous idea that God's infinite justice demands an infinite punishment.

Truly His ways are not as our ways; nor His thoughts as our thoughts. There are no visitations of God but those of mercy. War, famine, pestilence, as well as individual suffering and death, have no traces of the divine vengeance in their awful steps, but only those of the infernal spheres engendered by evil spirits and evil men.

These external punishments are sometimes terrible in the hells. Evil spirits hate and love to torture each other; and are continually experiencing the truth of the spiritual law, that whatever evil we design to inflict on others, rebounds, perhaps in a different shape, upon our own heads. Comparative order is maintained in the societies of hell only by fear and external bonds; for the sweet internal bonds of conscience, veneration, obedience to God and respect for others, have there no existence. The punishments inflicted by devils on each other are necessarily severe, for the repression of crime is there vastly more difficult than upon earth. Angels, indeed, are sometimes sent from heaven to mitigate their sufferings, and to restrain the violence of their mutual fury. Thus the Lord's love and pity abound unchangeably towards angels, men, and devils.

Well might the poor dying sinner, thinking of

the little golden sun of his village Sunday-school, and its beautiful motto of spiritual gold, exclaim: "I am afraid of man; but I am not afraid of God!"

Why, then, exclaims the oppressed soul—seeing the inrooted, organic nature of evil, and the inevitability of its self-inflicted punishment; and that God has no hidden hand or agency or secret purpose in any evil thing under the sun—why does not God annihilate the hells, stop the course of evil by violence, rid the world of it, and restore man to his primeval state, granting him a new beginning for a better end?

Have we always a clear and rational idea of the Omnipotence of God?

The power of God works entirely in harmony with the laws of His divine nature. It is indeed simply His laws in operation. His laws never change: His power is always the same: its manifestations being determined by our voluntary state towards Him. Live within and under the operation of His divine commandments, which are simply the laws of His own divine being, and He is all-powerful to save and bless you. But turn away from Him—and He does not and cannot deny you the power to do so—and all is changed

His blessings become curses, not on account of His will but of your nature. He cannot force you to accept His divine love. He cannot deliver you from the consequences of your sins, except by withdrawing you, with your own concurrence, from the sins themselves, or from the evil dispositions which lead to sin.

He cannot make a corrupt tree bring forth good fruit, because He cannot violate the laws of His own order. He cannot prevent a father from bequeathing hereditary evils to his child. He cannot even do His mighty works where there is unbelief. This inability of God to work contrary to the laws of His own existence, to be not God, is equally implied when we say that God cannot lie; He cannot change; He cannot repent; He cannot do evil or acquiesce in it; no, nor permit it in the sense of acquiescence.

Is it possible for God to annihilate any thing? It is the law or mode of His divine nature to create and bless. For Him to stop creating would be for Him to cease to be. How can He destroy and curse? If He does one thing at one time and the opposite at another, if His power is diverted into different channels by exigencies imposed upon Him by the conduct of man, He is not the Unchangeable—"the same yesterday, to-day, and for ever." Can you imagine the sun withdrawing his heat and light from a portion of the vegetable kingdom? God is one and indivisible and omnipresent. The same withdrawal of life which annihilated the hells, would annihilate the heavens and the universe. No. If there is cold and darkness anywhere in His creation, it is because some false medium, self-perverted, has intercepted the rays of the Divine Sun, which will shine on as before; and the cold and darkness must continue, until the medium, touched by the divine warmth, shall reopen his heart and receive it as in the beginning.

Suppose His power to destroy hell conceded; would it be wise or merciful in Him to do so? It is commonly supposed that the devils in hell would be very willing to be annihilated to escape their sufferings. This is a great mistake. Evil spirits congregate together by force of the great law of affinity, just as evil men do here. They have chosen their state, nor do they wish to leave it. If they were elevated into heaven, out of pure mercy, they would be suffocated like fish taken out of their own element into the air. Their sufferings come from their constant violations of the law of brotherly love. They enjoy the pursuit of their diabolical lusts as keenly and fiercely as the tiger does his raid on the village flock, or the hyena his meal in the village graveyard. Such, moreover, is the magical sphere of fantasy in which they are immersed, that they think themselves pre-eminently beautiful, wise, and great. It is only when the revealing light of heaven shines in upon them, that they discover what dreadful monsters they are, and call upon the rocks and the mountains to fall on them and hide them from what, in their moral darkness, they call "the wrath of the Lamb."

If it were possible with God and earnestly desired by the devils themselves, hell could not be annihilated without destroying the human race; nor could that be destroyed without involving the destruction of the heavens and the resolution of all into primeval chaos. This will sound strangely to those who are unacquainted with the structure of the spiritual universe, and the connection of one part with another, as revealed through Swedenborg. No portion of the universe stands alone, or isolated from the rest. There is no vacuum anywhere. The entire spiritual universe is based upon the physical, and flows into it as the soul into its body.

The physical universe was created first, and the

spiritual was built up afterwards as men by death became spirits and angels. The earth is the Lord's footstool, and our earth-life is the footstool or secret basis of our angelic life ever after. Such is the intimate connection between the spiritual and the natural, that if the latter were destroyed, the former would also be dissipated. "The earth is established for ever, so that it shall not be moved," says the Psalmist.

Are not the stars to fall from heaven and the earth to be destroyed at the Last Day? inquires the good Christian literalist. Ah, my friend! that heaven and earth are already passing away; and a new heaven and a new earth are being formed for the use of future and happier generations. The old heaven and the old earth on which Judgment has been given, and which are silently perishing, are the internal and the external or the spiritual and natural forms of the Apostolic Dispensation of Christianity; like the Jewish, a transitional state of the Lord's Church, preparing the basis for another and far grander evolution of Christian Truth and Life.

Why should the mere annihilation of hell destroy the human race? It seems to the uninstructed mind, that if the influx from hell were only withdrawn, man untempted would spontaneously return, or be easily restored to his original innocence and goodness. Swedenborg says that man's life, hereditary and acquired, is now so thoroughly perverted, that if the angelic life alone flowed into his interiors, he would be thrown into horrible torments, become insane, and finally perish. It was in this way probably that the whole Assyrian army was struck with blindness, and another one with frenzy; so that they turned each man upon the other. The hells are permitted to flow into us to keep us alive, and to maintain our mental equilibrium, our rationality, our liberty, our free-agency.

This will appear strange to those who know nothing of the spiritual side of psychology. Swedenborg, with all his advantages of spiritual observation, needed ocular demonstration of the fact. He saw a newly-arrived spirit from our world undergo the experiment of having his attendant evil spirits detached from him. The man, instead of appearing better and wiser and happier as we should have expected, fell down as if dead; nor could he think or feel or even breathe, until his communication with hell was restored. Such is the case with every one of us at this moment. Our very existence depends on an influx into us of life from the hells. And if the whole infernal world were destroyed, we should perish also.

We may make our external or acquired life as angelic as possible, so that no evil thing is ultimated through us; and still our hereditary evil, of which we are unconscious, is so vast that we can never remove it, and we are still connected by it through our attendant spirits with all the hells. We are only disjoined from hell after death by the wonderful processes of judgment and separation which occur in the world of spirits. Men and devils stand face to face, or side to side, and so communicate. Angels and devils by mutual divergence have become antipodal, and stand foot to foot. They do not communicate, but antagonize. In heaven only, "the wicked cease from troubling, and the weary are at rest."

The Lord, therefore, is not the cause of evil or its consequences. He does not permit it in the sense of acquiescing in or being satisfied with it. He does not use it as a means of promoting good; although his divine love never fails to educe from it the greatest good. He does not punish the authors and victims of it; but forgives them, pities them, loves them, and endeavors to deliver them from its bondage. He cannot prevent evil without destroying the free-agency of man and violating the laws of His own being. He cannot annihilate it in either devils or men, without destroying the physical and spiritual universe.

The soul need not shudder nor the heart sink at this clear, frank statement of the truth.

The Divine Love attracts all men to itself. "No man cometh unto me, except the Father which hath sent me draw him"—"And I, if I be lifted up from the earth, will draw all men unto me."

The Divine Truth "enlighteneth every man that cometh into the world." "In Thy light shall we see light."

The Lord Jesus Christ—this Divine Love and this Divine Wisdom in one Glorified Person—has established for us processes of cure and deliverance, so vast, so powerful, so certain, that not only may every human being be saved now from the power of sin, but the coming futures are golden with blissful promises of a perfect Church, an explained Word, a restored Eden, a sinless world, and an open Heaven. And even Hell will be reduced by self-inflicted sufferings to such a state of order and obedience, that although its inhabitants may have nothing but a vegetative existence, and be wrought into the Universal Temple as the sills and doorposts and paving stones of its fabric; yet there will be no pain, or sickness, or death, or sorrow, or crying, in the infinite, happy, peaceful, united Kingdom of the Lord.

Let us briefly recapitulate our positions, and see how sweet and serene a light the philosophy of Swedenborg throws even upon the darkest questions:

The Lord is Infinite Divine Love and Wisdom, and has none of the imperfect, anthropomorphic, or merely human qualities necessarily ascribed to Him in the letter of the Word.

He has no justice according to the popular import of that term,—for His love and justice are identical; nor does He regard our sins as crimes, offending his majesty and provoking his anger; but as terrible, self-inflicted misfortunes, exciting his infinite pity.

The free-agency of man is as necessary and fundamental as the self-existence of God; and the self-perverted Will of man is the source of all evil.

Evil is permitted to continue, because God cannot violate the free-agency of man,—the ground of his individuality, of his moral responsibility, and of the possibility of his final salvation.

The Lord alone lives. His Life, received into

good and orderly forms, produces all the good things in the universe; passing through evil or self-perverted forms, it is changed into all the evil things in the universe. Thus evil is its own punishment and tends always, through suffering and discipline, to its own abolition.

The Lord's love flows out to all alike, the good and the evil, the just and the unjust; and no evil thing we suffer can ever be attributed to Him, directly or indirectly, but always to ourselves or others, to evil men or evil spirits; for his providence is for ever leading men out of evil and not into it.

When we proceed to investigate the causes of suffering and death in the world, even the death of innocent little children, we shall take these shining truths along with us, and others drawn from the sacred storehouse of the Word, to dissipate the darkness of our natural minds, to correct our errors, and to still further "vindicate the ways of God to man." If we are made humble by painful revelations of our Inner Life, and grateful by continued manifestations of the Divine Goodness, we shall realize the truth and beauty of the poor Sunday-school scholar's religion,

"GOD IS LOVE."

CHAPTER IX.

WHY DID THEY DIE?

WHAT heart or mind was ever really satisfied with the reasons assigned by theologians for the death of children?

Who can believe that the Lord takes some infants away to save them from the evil to come, when He leaves others to grow up and become wicked men and finally lost spirits?

Or that He would ever punish any sin in the parent by tearing his child from him?

Or that the fearful suffering and mortality amongst our little ones, is in any way necessary to the welfare of His Church on earth, or to the order and strength of His heavenly kingdom?

What strange, unnatural, and irrational apologies does the human mind invent and fondly regard as reasons, when struggling to fortify itself in its foregone conclusion that the will of God is the cause of our bereavements? It seems hard to discriminate between the will of God and the volitions of evil men and evil spirits, the two great motor powers in the spiritual realm. What valid reason is there that the death of infants is any thing but one of the hideous effects of sin in the world, occurring in violation of divine order, like wars, pestilence, famine, disease in all its odious forms, catastrophes, robberies, assassinations, etc., etc.? Surely the Lord can have nothing to do in causing these terrible things. His divine vigilance must be for ever exercised to prevent, so far as possible, and to overrule for the best after the fact.

Cannot the New Church philosophy give us some strong and original light on this dark and difficult question, where all are bewildered and none satisfied? or if satisfied, only so by an unintelligent submission of the understanding to a faith to which the affections refuse to surrender.

Be it distinctly understood, that in this inquiry as to the causes of the death of children, we mean the primary, fundamental, or spiritual causes, and not the natural, physical, or proximate causes. These last are simply the media or agents through which the former operate. The natural causes are depraved constitutions inherited from parents, impure blood, improper food, atmospheric changes, filth, exposure, neglect, destructive medicines and all the errors of omission or commission which arise from the ignorance, carelessness, or folly of mankind. If all these causes were removed or rendered inoperative, no children would die; but that is impossible until the spiritual sphere of our life is restored to perfect order and beauty. Science can give our query only a superficial answer. For a true one we must penetrate the laws and phenomena of mind, and the correspondential relation between man and nature.

Swedenborg's theory of causation is novel, complete, and self-sustaining; based on the Word of God, and answering the intuitions of the highest reason. Some of its elements in fragmentary form, have cropped out here and there in the greatest thoughts of the greatest thinkers in different ages; but it comes from him as a grand whole, not invented by himself, but discovered to him in the light of that Spiritual World into which his mind had been lifted.

He teaches dogmatically, "from things heard and seen," as he himself states it; not from subtile imaginings or speculations. He does not debate whether there is a soul or a vital force or a distinct will and understanding, each with specific properties. He affirms his positions; because he has been favored with an inside view: he has seen the vital machinery at work as no living man has ever seen it. He therefore uses simple narrative, not logic and rhetoric; except that highest logic and rhetoric involved in the statement of truth, of which beauty and symmetry are the essential qualities.

He differentiates his philosophy from all others by a fundamental axiom.

All causes exist in the spiritual world: their effects simultaneously or successively in the natural world; and the two worlds are connected by the correspondence existing between the spiritual causes and the natural effects.

Men have hitherto sought for causes on the same level or plane with the effects; and of course have discovered nothing but coincident effects, apparent causes. Heat and light, they say, are the causes of vegetation; the sun is the cause of heat and light; but they are silent when asked the cause of the sun. Fever is the cause of death, malaria the cause of fever, decaying matter the cause of malaria, and so on, until they are driven to the material limit of observation and to silence again.

What should we think of philosophers who surveyed the terrible débris of a battle-field, and in seeking for the causes of the strange scene, busied themselves with mechanical concussions, momenta of bodies, solutions of continuity, and other physical phenomena, ignoring entirely the mighty whirlwinds of human passion which had made the forms and forces of nature the mere agents of their will!

When men will obstinately tread the old fruitless circle of natural investigation, living and thinking always in the sphere of effects; when they shrink back at the threshold of the spiritual world, and scout the investigation of spiritual things; we can understand the assertion of Swedenborg, that the angels looking down into the minds of men see nothing but thick darkness. If they have no spiritual light in them, how can they be seen?

Swedenborg begins with the Divine Being or First Cause, and traces from Him the secondary causes in the spiritual sphere, and their corresponding effects or apparent causes in the natural sphere.

A spiritual Sun, the first Proceeding or Emanation of the divine sphere, representing the Lord in the spiritual world, is the cause of the natural sun representing the Lord in nature.

The emanations from the spiritual Sun are Love and Wisdom, which are the causes of the corresponding heat and light emanating from the natural sun, and exhibit corresponding properties.

Spiritual affinities determining spiritual forms and organizations, are the real causes of chemical affinities, the supposed natural cause of that atomic arrangement which determines the properties of bodies.

The various passions, emotions, perceptions, thoughts, etc., of the spiritual spheres, are the causes of all the various animals, plants, and minerals in the world.

The spiritual Progressions of the Church in man, are the causes of the Evolutions of Human History.

These are given merely as general examples of the laws by which the spiritual and the natural worlds co-exist and correspond. Each of them would require a volume for its elucidation. These laws are not to be proven by the accumulation of evidence as in matters of natural science. Superior things cannot be seen from inferior things; internal from external; spiritual from natural; but the reverse. Grasp the idea of spiritual causes and their relation to each other, and natural phenomena are lighted up with a new beauty and splendor. The Invisible and the Visible are seen to run parallel to each other; one the life, the other the form; one the soul, the other the body; through the greatest things and the least, from the all-cheering sun to the minutest flower-leaf and dew-drop.

The poet calls his beloved one a rose or a lily. It seems to us a mere comparison; but it may be far more. It may be symbolical, or an expression of the true relations of cause and effect between the inner and the outer worlds. The sweet and pure ideas blossoming up in virgin souls are the living causes of all the flowers in the world. The Lord's love and wisdom flowing into a beautiful spiritual form, the virgin soul, produces a radiant sisterhood of graceful and charming thoughts. That is the spiritual or causative side. The sun's heat and light representing the divine love and wisdom, flowing into a rose-bush representing the virgin mind, causes it to bloom full of fragrant roses representing the beautiful sisterhood of charming thoughts. That is the natural side of the spiritual picture. Thus substance and shadow run side by side mirroring each other, the invisible things of the creation being made known by the things that are visible.

The sum total of the good, beautiful, and useful things in the outer world is the sum total of the good, wise, and useful operations of the aggregate Human Soul. The sum total of the evil, ugly, and destructive things in nature, is the sum total of the disorderly spiritual activities of the same soul. Each human being, daily and hourly contributes his share to the aggregate good or evil in human nature; and through that medium by correspondential influx, to all the good or evil forces and forms which we see in the physical world. The poorest, humblest Christian on earth, who cannot contribute even a mite to the treasury, can make the grass grow and the flowers bloom for the benefit of others, by the cultivation of gentle affections and pure thoughts in his own soul. It is the righteous alone who save the cities of our earth, day by day, from the fate of Sodom and Gomorrah.

This is not poetry but fact, and fact of the deepest significance. We cannot point out the exact uses or beauties in the outer realm, of which this or that man or woman is the efficient cause. We cannot say, too, of this or that particle of food, that it shall make this or that portion of the blood, or build up such or such an organ and tissue. Every thing is received into a general reservoir, taken to the central heart, and redistributed under universal laws, according to the necessities and affinities of even remotest and minutest atom. So it is in the spiritual realm, for the aggregate Human Soul is also in the human form. If no sweet and pure thoughts represented by roses, were to be contributed to the aggregate Human Mind, the roses would necessarily disappear from the world. The beautiful and the unbeautiful, the good and the evil, continually fluctuate in the physical sphere, corresponding to the fluctuations of the spiritual in man; and thence arises the hope of the final extinction of all unlovely things.

This relation between the spiritual and the natural is finely illustrated in one of the most obscure and remarkable miracles recorded in the Word. Our Lord is about casting out a legion of devils from a poor, naked, weeping and self-mutilated lunatic. The devils beseech Him earnestly to permit them to enter into a great herd of swine feeding near by. He consents; and the swine, losing the instinct of self-preservation, rush violently down a steep place and are drowned in the sea. The appearance here is, that the spiritual bodies of devils entered into the physical bodies of swine and drove them madly to their destruction. A different but corresponding scene occurred on the other side of the veil.

The swine represented the selfish and greedy

principles in the man's mind, which had invited the devils to make a lodgment there. At that age it is well known that devils had broken from the hells and were crowding up into the world of spirits, where every man is as to his spirit, and were thence taking possession of the souls and bodies of men. This was one of the causes which necessitated the Lord's incarnation. The Lord's work in this seeming miracle was to deliver the man from the bondage of those selfish and greedy lusts, so that he might sit at his feet "clothed and in his right mind." The devils beg to be permitted to retire into the hells whence they came, and to remain in the undisturbed enjoyment of their own similar lusts. The Lord consents; the greedy and sensual devils leave the man and rush into their hells, rejoicing to escape the presence of the Lord. The spiritual transaction is represented in the phenomenal field of nature by the herd of swine rushing headlong into the sea.

So to-day, if the tiger-element, the wolf-element, the snake-element, the vulture-element in the human heart, could be removed entirely and at once by some miraculous power, all of those obnoxious creatures would immediately disappear from the face of the earth.

Understand clearly, that no spiritual forces can act or flow outwardly into nature except through their corresponding natural forms. The soul can only act through the brain, the corresponding natural form of its affections and thoughts. The Lord's love cannot operate in creation until it has assumed the natural form of heat. Evil spheres may precipitate themselves upon man, but they cannot induce bodily disease, until they obtain a corresponding basis or fulcrum in atmospheric changes, improper food, malaria, or some organic virus. The fallacy of the sensuous thinker lies in supposing that the brain, the sun's heat, or the malaria, has some natural force or power of itself, independent and separate from the spiritual forces which organized and sustained it.

Before attempting to give spiritual reasons for the existence of disease and early death by the light of Correspondence, we will illustrate the wonderful power of that knowledge, now restored for the reconstruction of Human Thought, by tracing to their true spiritual causes the two greatest evils of the world, incontinence and intemperance; the original fountain-heads of disease and death; against which reason, science, religion, and law have warred in vain, because man has never detected the secret sources from which they spring.

The Religious Idea in man makes what is called the Church. Every man, says Swedenborg, is a Church in its least form. Churches are societies of men having various Religious Ideas—those of the same society holding similar ideas. The great invisible, universal, catholic Church of God includes all men who have any Religious Ideas whatever. They are arranged spiritually into one great whole by the Lord; those who receive most good and truth from Him occupying the centre; those who receive less come next; and so on in exact gradation; until those who receive least or almost none are placed in the remote circumference. Those who have the Word of God and are in the greatest light, are compared by Swedenborg to the heart and lungs in the human body, which are the great centres for the distribution of life, heat, motion, and power to all the rest.

The Lord's vital influx is first into the Church and from the Church into the world; first into the Religious Idea of the individual, and thence into his more exterior organization. And the secret, interior, spiritual history of the Church,—which is so multiform externally and is seen as One only by the

Lord,—is the key to all the evolutions of History and of the entire life of man, composite or unitary. Such as the Church in man is, such will the world be.

The Lord declares that He is the Bridegroom and the Church is His Bride. This is not a metaphor or a simile, or some vague poetical way of stating the case. It is the most beautiful and momentous fact in the universe. Affections and thoughts always go in married pairs. A man loves what he thinks and thinks what he loves. The Divine Truth or Wisdom is the Bridegroom. Pure and heavenly affections or emotions, received from the Lord, constitute the heart of the Church in man. The conjunction of the Divine Wisdom with these heavenly affections is the Heavenly Marriage, the mystical union of the Bridegroom and the Bride, of the Lord and His Church. This heavenly marriage is the type, origin, and cause of the holy sacrament called marriage upon earth, in which by two being made one flesh, a perfect union of the will and the understanding is contemplated; the will of each party making one with the understanding of the other.

The Church is married to the Lord when it knows Him truly, and delights to love, honor, and obey Him; when it thinks His thoughts and does His will, and ever looks to Him and to Him alone. What is true of the Church universal is true of each individual, or of the Church in its smallest form. A perfect image of this Heavenly Marriage, this perfect fidelity and chastity, exists in the relation of husband and wife among the angels. It is the model or pattern for our earthly endeavor; but we can never attain to it until we know the true God as angels do, and turn our affections or will into eternal harmony with His Wisdom, Truth, Light, and Law.

This conjunction of the affections of man with the truths of the Lord's wisdom is the spiritual cause of the conjugial love in the sexes; that pure, chaste, undying, heavenly passion, possible only between two; which in its turn is the fountain of all the domestic and social loves that animate, unite, enlighten, and beautify human society. The possibility of this heavenly love in man depends upon the approximation he makes to a true knowledge of God, and the unition of the affections of his heart with the truths he has received in his understanding.

Spiritual adultery is the primal cause of natural adultery. The alienation of the heart's affections from the true God, and their concentration upon other and false and unworthy objects of love and worship, destroys or deteriorates the Church or Religious Idea in man, perverts the conjugial principle at its very origin, darkens the understanding, and transfers the domination of our whole nature to the sensual powers, which were designed to occupy the last and lowest places,—to be the servants, not the masters of the rest. When the affections are turned from the true God, they turn also from the true wife; when they are fixed upon spiritual evils and falsities, they are fixed also on the painted harlots who exteriorly represent them. Thus it is that spiritual adultery is the cause of natural adultery, and of all unchastity in the sexual relations.

Therefore the very first commandment, the first in place and the first in importance, forbids the precedence of any Ruling Love before that of the Lord himself. Whatever a man loves supremely is his god: the central point of his universe to which every thing in the circumference refers itself. If he supremely loves the Lord, the whole man from centre to circumference is a miniature form of heaven, and the purest love and the brightest wisdom flame and sparkle downward into the commonest act of his beneficent and happy life. On the other hand, Self, the World, Riches, Power, Fame, Pleasure, and other strange idols, are the reigning divinities in every human heart, from whose central throne the Lord is excluded. The nature of their government and the effect of their worship, are they not written in the tears, the blood, the lusts, the folly, and the madness of the world?

Spiritual adultery is the great burden of the denunciations of the Prophets against the Jewish Church. The whoredoms of Israel, their love of other gods than the Lord, was the central cause of all their sins, miseries, and final destruction. Their spiritual adultery became so grievous that the union of the Divine Wisdom with the Jewish Church could only be represented outwardly, and thereby maintained in fact and reality, by the Prophet of the Lord taking to his embrace an adulterous woman. Hosea affirms:

"Then said the Lord unto me: Go yet, love a woman beloved of her friend, yet an adulteress; according to the love of the Lord toward the children of Israel, who look to other gods and love flagons of wine."

"So I bought her to me for fifteen pieces of

silver and for a homer of barley and a half homer of barley!

"And I said unto her, 'Thou shalt abide for me many days. Thou shalt not play the harlot, and thou shalt not be for another man: so will I also be for thee.'"

One of the immediate consequences of looking to other gods is to "love flagons of wine:" and therein lies the secret of intemperance. This is not clear to those who think only from sensuous grounds, and do not know the relation of cause and effect existing between the will and the understanding. The will flows into the understanding by interior ways; and whatever takes place in its sphere is repeated in a corresponding intellectual form in the understanding. Perverted or corrupt affections in the will produce false ideas or thoughts in the intellectual plane. This is the real origin of all the false doctrines in the world. Men see with the mind what they wish to see with the heart. Belief of the truth "with the heart" is saving faith; and no other is saving.

The confused, disorderly, and false condition of the whole intellectual sphere, when it draws its life from evil affections and selfish passions, is spiritual drunkenness. The man sees nothing rightly or in the right place. His understanding is darkened: his rational faculties blunted: his senses even report falsely: and yet his self-love is so active and so unregulated by reason, that he esteems himself wisest, greatest, and best, when heavenly light would reveal him to be in the most shocking and pitiable mental state.

Swedenborg's definition of a spiritual drunkard is, "one who believes nothing but what he can understand from things sensual, scientific or philosophical." When we reflect that such is the exact mental state of so large a part of the thinking world, can we wonder that natural drunkenness abounds in all countries? Babylon, making the whole earth drunken, is interpreted by Swedenborg's spiritual law to mean that the lust of spiritual dominion, or the love of ruling over the minds of men, has so falsified the truths of the Church, that it has filled the intellectual sphere with errors, fallacies and insanities. And to show the secret interior connection between spiritual adultery and spiritual drunkenness, the Word declares that the wine with which Babylon made the nations drunk, was "the wine of the wrath of her fornication."

Whatever is transacted in the soul always repeats and perpetuates itself in correspondential forms in the body. The spiritual drunkenness of the race, a state of errors, fantasies, and hallucinations on all subjects, is the real cause of the morbid craving for intoxicating drinks and poisonous drugs which affects mankind. It is a desire to get away from the sphere of realities and practical duties, and to conjure up around them a fantastic, unreal world, where their selfish loves can have full play and power. Evil spirits finally get full possession of their victims; and the horrors of delirium tremens are subdued but genuine pictures of the methods by which the lost souls delight to terrify and torture each other.

The effect of this spiritual drunkenness in stupefying the soul, until the voices of Prophet and Seer are disregarded, and the Word of God becomes unintelligible to the Church and the world, is finely stated by Isaiah:

"Stay yourselves and wonder: cry ye out, and cry: They are drunken, but not with wine: they stagger, but not with strong drink."

"For the Lord hath poured out upon you the spirit of deep sleep, and hath closed your eyes; the prophets, and your rulers, the seers hath he covered."

"And the vision of all is become unto you as

the words of a book that is sealed, which men deliver to one that is learned, saying, Read this, I pray thee : and he saith, I cannot, for it is sealed :

"And the book is delivered to him that is not learned, saying, Read this, I pray thee: and he saith, I am not learned."

What a photographic picture of the present state of the Christian world, taken by the son of Amoz, through the mystic camera of Prophecy, more than two thousand years ago!

Idolatry then, or the supreme love of any person, thing, or principle other than the true God, is the cause of those emotional perversions, which eventuate in polygamy, concubinage, and all the various forms of licentiousness. These emotional perversions are in turn the causes of the intellectual perversions characterized as falsities. Thus evil affections and false ideas are the fountains whence flow the sensual appetites, the beastly gluttony and intemperance in all things, which have cursed the world with misery, disease, and painful death.

It may be here objected that many a man is perfectly chaste in his habits, who worships a false god of some kind with all his heart and soul. Also that thousands of persons are distinguished for temperance, whose minds are dark as ocean caves with all sorts of false doctrine. This proves nothing; for the sphere of good and evil are so mixed in this world, that the interiors and exteriors do not correspond. Many a beautiful soul is here resident in a deformed body, and many a cruel, guileful spirit in a perfect one; but this will be reversed by and by.

Men are governed also by external restraints; restraints of law, manners and customs or the usages of society, by the ceremonial restraints of religion, by the authority of others, by fear of the loss of health, money, or reputation, and other external motives, which withhold them from the indulgence or ultimation of evil passions which really lie concealed in their hearts. Moreover a man may have all the elements of unchastity and drunkenness in his spiritual nature, and still his ruling love of power or riches or position may so dominate his character, that nothing licentious or intemperate may ever appear in his external conduct.

Nevertheless all men who worship false gods and cherish as truths the mere falsifications of truth, are spiritually adulterous and intemperate; and will be found to be so, when they put off their exteriors at death, and come into their interior and real life.

They will have no genuine regard for the marriage relation, and no belief in its pre-eminent bearing upon the order, beauty, and peace of the spiritual universe. All, however, who have restrained their appetites from religious principle will receive new life, new affection, new thought from the Lord, and with them a genuine, voluntary, eternal spirit of chastity and temperance, such as the angels enjoy.

All endeavors to exterminate these terrible evils will be vain, unless the blow be struck at their roots. Those roots are not in the natural and sensual appetites of man, which ought to be amended and purified by the enlightened restraints of law, reason, and religion. Such is the erroneous doctrine of philanthropists, who lop away at the leaves and branches, whilst the tree of iniquity draws its secret life and vigor from an undiscovered fountain. The root is in the heart and brain of the Christian Church. With all its love, its patience, its zeal, its consecration, it will labor in vain through the night of ages, until it discovers its error, and at the command of the Lord casts its net "upon the right side of the ship,"

When the Lord Jesus Christ is worshiped as the Supreme God, and the old idea of Him as a subordinate and interceding Son is lost in the blaze of His recognition as our Heavenly Father; when the Word of God is no longer a sealed book to both clergy and laity, but an open Oracle uttering its priceless treasures of angelic wisdom to all men; a Fountain in which ever-present Angels never cease to stir the Living Waters; the heart and brain of the Church on earth will become so united to the heart and brain of the Church in heaven, that the Conjugial Life will become as possible to men as to angels; and the fire of the divine love and the light of the divine wisdom will pass down through the purified senses of a regenerate Church to deliver and redeem the world!

Then shall the ears of all men hear in reality what the beloved Apostle heard in vision:

"As it were the voice of a great multitude, and as the voice of many waters, and as the voice of mighty thunderings, saying—'Alleluia, for the Lord God omnipotent reigneth.'"

Here it may be well to note, before coming nearer to the question we are to answer, how we are saved from the sins of the will and the errors of the understanding by Prayer and Faith. Prayer is emotional; faith is intellectual. Prayer turns the affections toward God, thus bringing our wills into harmony with His Divine Will. Faith turns the intellect to Him, and submits the understanding to the operation of Divine Truth. Prayer is the heart, faith the light, of the garden of the soul. No matter how good the seed or how rich the soil, there will be neither blossom nor fruit, unless prayer and faith, like descending angels, bring down to us the heat and light of the Divine Sun.

Why do we clamor at the gate of heaven like unruly beggars, supplicating for this or that earthly blessing? Think you we shall be heard for our "much speaking?" Does not our Heavenly Father know what we have need of before we ask Him? Can we illumine His mind or refresh His memory or change His intentions? Alas! when these "long prayers," these "vain repetitions," full of self and selfishness, are not answered, we are ready to accuse the Lord of deafness and blindness, and to fall into fearful doubts and despairs.

But genuine prayer?—

Genuine prayer is humility, even to the total abnegation of self, and the turning of the affections toward the Lord alone. The change effected by it is altogether in ourselves. It is a condition of the spiritual organism. When the Lord's love is permitted to flow into us and through us, it brings with it all the blessings we can receive or bear. Prayer, then, is no frenzied wrestling with Jehovah to compel His ear or induce His favor. It is merely opening the door of the heart. How sweet! how simple!—

"Behold! I stand at the door and knock."

In exploring the spiritual causes of incontinence and intemperance, the typical fountains of all disease, we have not receded from our subject, but are approaching it. We have rather discovered the mouths of the mephitic caverns, whose horrible exhalations have poisoned the atmosphere of the world. All diseases, like every object and motion in the natural world, are representative of spiritual things; and if we could read their symbolism as we do a book, we would get at the whole story of moral and intellectual perversions, of evil and its ravages on the spirit of man.

If no sin had appeared in the world there would have been no disease or painful death; because no moral law having been violated, there would have been no corresponding natural causes of disease. Swedenborg saw in the evil portion of the spiritual world all the terrible elements of our diseases, although not a single natural object, law, or cause existed there for their generation; and he saw them communicated in many instances to the human body. Our Lord moreover recognized the infernal world as the true source of our diseases, when He cured all manner of morbid affections—the whole pathological catalogue—by simply casting out the evil spirits who had induced and fixed them on the sufferers.

The Christian philosophy nominally attributes all natural evils, including sickness and death, to sin. But it has lost the connecting link between the moral disorders and the physical disorders which afflict us. It fails to show how sin produces its objective miseries. It ignores spiritual causes, and explains every thing by natural causes almost as persistently as the materialist does. It cannot understand how the worship of strange gods causes adultery; how the falsification of truth produces a passion for strong drink; how burning lusts produce burning fevers; how loss of spiritual nerve-life in the church produces paralysis among men; how every sin has its exact outburst and symbol in the sufferings and sorrows of humanity; and how there are cancers and plagues and hydrophobias of the soul, the secret causes of those horrible diseases in the body. Nothing but the knowledge of correspondences can make all these things plain.

The materialist thinks he has accounted for diseases by saying that they are the effects of the violation of natural laws. But what are natural laws? They are physical embodiments or expressions of moral or divine laws, just as heat is the physical form of the Divine Love, and a rose the physical expression of a delicate thought. The spiritual and the natural are inseparable. No matter how good or wise a man may interiorly be, if he violates knowingly or unknowingly what we call a natural law, he immediately subjects himself to the influx of those evil spirits who delight in the violation of its corresponding spiritual law, and disease may be induced upon him.

The spiritual side to the philosophy of medicine is a subject for the wiser future. A positive scientific basis must be first laid for it by observation and experiment; just as the earth had to be constructed before its destined inhabitant, man, could take form upon it. We know little with certainty at present, except the general law, that evil spheres or exhalations from the hells and from the spiritual forms of men, co-operating with correspondential disorderly movements or perverted objects in nature, produce various morbid effects on the human body, even to the degree of destroying its texture, so that it is no longer capable of containing the corresponding soul.

It is the business of the physician to study both the spiritual and natural sides of these strange phenomena: the spiritual side at least may well engage the attention of the theologian and the Christian. He will discover that an atmosphere of spiritual malaria, more or less dense and dark, encompasses and emanates from every community, society, church, government and institution among men. Every human being by each act of licentiousness, intemperance, falsehood, injustice, cruelty or any other crime, contributes his share to these vast volumes of evil and falsity, which descend upon every human habitation, and combining with the putrid exhalations of nature become the seeds and souls of pestilence and death.

Let us not be deceived, nor invest this dark subject with more mystery than it possesses. Let us not attribute to the mysterious designs and inscrutable workings of Divine Providence, causes which are so easily traceable to our own doors. Every unchaste thought we have nurtured, every resentful feeling, every contemptuous expression, every base and unworthy passion, has projected from us a spiritual exhalation, which became a part of the direful causes that blighted the harvests and flooded the rivers; lit the torch of conflagration and overwhelmed the traveler on his way; planted the seed of pestilence in the earth, and loosened the bloodhounds of war; brought the worm to the rose of beauty, and robbed the mother of her child.

We violate all the commandments of God; we live in utter forgetfulness of his presence or indifference to his will; we permit our lower natures to dominate the higher; our souls, perverted by evils both hereditary and acquired, are miniatures of hell; we are connected interiorly with myriads of subtle spirits more wicked than ourselves; and our combined spheres radiate forth the most terrible spiritual poisons which render active the similar forms of nature: and still we stand aghast at the plagues which ravage our cities, the social evils which corrupt society, and the angels of death that desolate our hearthstones. In our moral blindness we even persuade ourselves that these curses are blessings in disguise—the visitations or providences or messengers of God!

Death! What a complex phenomenon! Who can unravel its mysteries? What curious processes are going on invisible to the natural eye! The body is undergoing organic changes which will soon unfit it for the residence of the soul. The soul herself withdraws her banners from the outer walls and retires to a citadel unseen. Two angels who had followed it from birth, are withdrawing into heaven, and kiss their sweet farewells from the opening gates of pearl. Two evil spirits who had beset it during life, are being driven back into their hells, and a whirlwind of suffering and anguish issues from the yawning pit.

Another tableau; and the angels are gone; the soul is asleep; the devils are sinking into the abyss, reflecting their own horrible struggles and gaspings upon the dying body; and then! some poor human bereaved ones are weeping over a corpse!

Nor is that all. The glorious angels in a day or two gladly welcome their earth-friend to his heavenly home, and show him the wonderful panorama of his own regenerate life. The human mourners in the desolate house treasure up the garments, the pictures, the memory; the faded garlands of the feast, after the lights have gone and the guests departed. The devils enter into the worms and deface the sacred temple of the body, scowling at humanity to the last through the skull and cross-bones of the grave.

How can these evil spiritual spheres affect infants and little children, in whom no actual evils of life have ever been developed? Do not spheres of innocence and peace shine through them from the Lord? Are they not protected from devils by these spheres, which torture the evil ones who approach?

Yes—as to the spirit. No evil spirit approaches the little one to excite the least evil or falsity. The child has no moral or intellectual life of its own. It is not good, however; for the choice of good or evil has not yet arisen in the will, or the power of analysis in the understanding. No evil thing can find any basis for its influx into any emotions or thoughts or actions of the little, feeble, slowly-developing creature.

And still there is a basis in that child for the influx of evil spheres—so broad, so vast, so dreadful, that half of the human race perish in early infancy.

Our Lord descended upon earth; was born of woman; suffered as we do; was tempted of devils; was overwhelmed with sorrows, until He sweat as it were "great drops of blood;" was crucified and gave up the ghost in darkness and agony. He was perfect innocence, perfect goodness, perfect wisdom.

How could the hells approach Him? How could any evil spirits assault Him? How could He suffer and die as we do? The answer to these questions will show us why little children perish, whilst their sweet little faces are shining with the spheres of innocence and peace.

We all have adjoined to us an hereditary nature which is wholly evil. This is the accumulated evil and falsity of our whole ancestry. We are born into this evil form: it connects us with the hells: it instigates us to evil as soon as we can think and feel in any determinate manner. We are not responsible for it, except as we make some of it our own by leading the evil lives of some of our ancestors. It is in this way that grandfathers return in their grandchildren. It is in this way that the children's teeth are set on edge, because the fathers have eaten sour grapes. This hereditary evil is transcribed and symbolized in the structure of the infant body. Not a fibre, not a muscle, not a globule of blood, not a lineament, not a hair, but bears the infinitesimal physical traces of deviation from divine order, and becomes the means or basis of the influx of spiritual malaria into the organism on the least exciting cause.

The soul comes from the father, the body from

the mother; and the latter bears, transcribed into it from both parents, the entire hereditary principle. The soul of Jesus Christ was Jehovah God—the Supreme Being, the Father. In accepting a human body from woman, He took on Himself our hereditary nature, invested Himself as it were with the evil and false principles of the whole race. This is represented by His genealogy given in Scripture, every name standing for whole genera and species of hereditary evils. This brought Him into contact with all the hells. This permitted them to flow into Him and incite Him intensely to every evil of which man has ever been guilty. He was without sin. No evil desire or thought was ever permitted to triumph. He cast them all out. He purified His sensuous nature from all dross. He subdued the hereditary nature, so as to acquire a Divine Humanity, in which He ascended to heaven, and in which He ever stands ready to deliver us from any conceivable evil, hereditary or acquired, into which we may be plunged. Thus He is "the Way"—"the Resurrection"—and "the Life."

This hereditary evil sphere is "the Canaanite in the land," which we are commanded to exterminate, and against which we wage a continued but ineffectual warfare. We advance in regeneration by putting away our evil states of life. It is a painful combat, because we love our evils and cling to them, straining our understandings to the utmost to excuse and defend them. When at last we feel ourselves getting rid of them, we enter to our dismay into states of pious exaltation and spiritual pride, and we find the new evils worse than the old. The combat is endless. We can never become good—never. We may cut off the tree of evil at the ground, but the roots are indestructible, springing up for ever from the abyss of hell.

How shall we be saved from this terrible nightmare of spiritual death? The New Church does not credit, nor does the Word of God authorize, those theological mysticisms—the angry Father, the atoning Son, the imputation of righteousness by an act of faith. All that is incomprehensible to those who acknowledge only one God—the Lord Jesus Christ—shining for ever in his Glorified Human Body. When we feel ourselves sinking into hell, we stretch out our hands to the Divine Man who walks upon the sea, and cry with Peter, "Help, Lord, or we perish!" His Divine Human nature, purified, glorified in every hereditary principle, imparts unto us its own power, and we are saved, not from the penalty of sin, but from the bondage of sin itself. We lose our hereditary selfish life, and receive a new and higher life from the Lord

Infants perish, then, by the influx of evil spiritual spheres into the sphere of hereditary evil, which has its basis in the physical structure of the infantile body. But what is it that excites these spheres into such fatal activity? Here again, as in the case of licentiousness and intemperance, we trace the real cause to the heart of the Church, or the state of the Religious Idea in the universal and the individual man. Here also we can only see the cause by the light of correspondence. It is the early and rapid destruction of the states of innocence and peace, which the Lord is continually infusing into His Church as the vital means of its regeneration. The Lord is daily being born into our hearts as the infant Jesus, coming to take on himself our hereditary evils and save us from them. But the Herod of our perverted natures, refusing His reign, indignantly commands the slaughter of the innocents; and our Bethlehems are filled with mourning.

When will these things cease? When will infants and little children escape these terrible trials and sufferings, and live to vigorous and joyous manhood and womanhood? Whenever there is a

Church in the world and in the heart of man, which retains its own innocent and beautiful childhood to old age; when there are no adult faces marked with pride and hatred and sensuality; when the lion and the lamb feed together; when the service of God is no longer the gorgeous ceremonials of Chief Priests and Scribes, but the sweet hosannas of little children strewing green branches in His way!

If the divine life flowing through the universal mind of man produces all the phenomena of the outward world, historical, social, and physical; if the good and beautiful and useful things correspond to the divine life flowing through good hearts; and the evils around us correspond to the same life flowing through evil and wicked souls; why is it that each does not always get his own exact correspondential surroundings? Why is it that the wicked ever prosper and are in power, or that the righteous are ever cast down and forsaken? Why is it that vice ever flaunts in purple, or virtue ever cowers in rags? Why are the garments of the Angel of Death ever red with the blood of the Innocents?

No one can doubt that all this is the result of spiritual disorder. It is one of the manifestations of hell on earth. In heaven the angel desires to give all he has to others; to break every yoke; to lift every burden; to share every sorrow. He never wishes to impose his will or his opinions upon others. He leaves every one in perfect freedom, and is himself the servant of all. But spirits in hell and unregenerate men on earth are full of self-love, and of jealousy, hatred, contempt or indifference toward others. They delight to absorb and not to give. They impose, so far as they can, their will, their opinions, their sorrows, their burdens upon others. They attempt to absorb others' individuality; to appropriate their services, giving them nothing in return; and to tyrannize over them in every way possible. The tendency of the evil sphere is to fasten itself like a leech or a vampire upon others; and whilst drawing their life out of them, to cast upon them its own foul exhalations and its own horrible shadow.

Hence the questions of life and providence become so obscure and complex. If each soul were isolated from others, or if the life and laws of heaven prevailed amongst men, the surroundings, fate, and fortune of each individual would be seen to be the perfect counterpart of his interior being. Unregenerate men are all slaves; they do not love nor try to serve others. The bondage we endure from the domination of others, evil men and evil spirits, would be appalling and intolerable if we were made all at once conscious of our chains. Hence the painful confusion of the effects or outbirths which fall upon the good and the evil, the innocent and the guilty. Hence we can trace no man's secret thread of life, and say why he suffers this or enjoys that, any more than we can follow a single drop of the ocean water in its course round the world. God alone knows all, and overrules all for the best consistently with his own eternal laws of wisdom and order.

The sweetest word in the language, next to Love, is Liberty. God and his angels alone respect the perfect freedom of man. It is the continual effort of the Lord to deliver us from ourselves, our enemies and our friends; and to bring us into a simple, frank and voluntary relation to Himself alone. This is the glorious liberty wherewith Christ maketh free. To shake off the yoke of spirits and devils; to put our own evil passions and falsities under foot; to receive from others and to give to them nothing but the reflected love and wisdom of the Lord; to identify cordially our own wills and lives with His will and life and with no others; this is to know and love the true God "whose service is perfect freedom."

Swedenborg affirms that the Lord predestinates all men to heaven; yet all are not saved. He predestinates all men to be crowned with blessings from the cradle to the grave; yet few or none attain such felicity. He predestinates all men to live to the rounded maturity of human life; yet a large majority of them do not number half their allotted days. If man had not sinned, says Swedenborg, he would have lived without disease, and expired in a serene old age without a particle of suffering. The Lord's will, then, has not been done in the earth. The deaths of children are not providences, but they result from the violations of divine law. The Lord does not provide for the death of little children. He simply permits it, as he does a thousand other calamities which He cannot prevent without infringing upon the free-agency of man. To suppose that He wills the suffering and death of children, would be something near akin to that article in the faith of the past Dispensation, thus expressed by one of its advocates: "That God did, *de facto*, inflict the highest torments on an innocent, pure, spotless creature, even the human nature of his own Son." The New Churchman, however, may discover that the sufferings of Christ and the sufferings of little children can be clearly traced to identical causes, and that God had no active share in either. Yet as He permitted the former, because He could not, consistently with the freedom with which He had endowed man, prevent them, so does He permit the latter—seeking, however, continually to avert them; and when this cannot be done, to overrule them for good.

Nor are we robbed of any genuine consolation by tracing our sorrows and bereavements to their true source, the evil spheres of evil spirits and men, including especially our own. We are greatly comforted by the thought that God is not the author of our woes. We are delighted to learn that our calamities all result from violations of His will—that they are not sent of God. We have clearer, sweeter, heavenlier views of the Lord as our ever-sympathizing Friend and Father. We know that, before and after affliction alike, He gives us all the good we can receive, never changing His plan nor forgetting our weakness. And we know that if we shun evils as sins against Him, He will finally deliver us from the power of evil, and will safely unite us to those we love in His heavenly kingdom.

How much more closely are we drawn to our Heavenly Father, how much more sweetly are we consoled, when we take a true view of the providence of the Divine Love! When we note in our calamities and sorrows the trail of the serpent! When we start from their ghastly presences, hating evil as never before, and smiting our own breasts as "miserable sinners!" When we turn for light and peace and consolation to the Lord, with the eager, loving, trusting spirit of Martha, when she rushed into the presence of her Great Friend, exclaiming:

"Lord! if thou hadst been here, my brother had not died."

Yes. In His presence are life and health and strength and "fullness of joy." He does not take away the jewels that He gave. If we lose them, it is through our own folly or ignorance or disobedience, or the malign influence that radiates from the hearts of other sinful men and evil spirits. Nor are they really lost, but only removed from the sensuous sphere and from our outward view. And if we are willing to forsake all and follow our Divine Lord and Master, He will in due time restore to us every one of our blessings, exalted and increased a hundred-fold.

CHAPTER X.

WHAT GOOD CAN COME OF IT?

THE Lord's Providence is in all things, the greatest and the least. He notes the fall of a sparrow, and numbers the hairs of our heads. He leads us by ways unknown to ourselves. Gently He draws us from evil to good. He showers blessings upon us at every step of life, both before and after every one of its afflictions and trials. So great and visible is the spiritual good frequently derived from the direst calamities, that we are almost led to believe that they were merely links in a vast chain of beneficent designs. The heart clings fondly to the thought that the will of God has been done in all the events of life, and that everything is ordered for the best.

Nothing happens, however, for the best, but that which occurs in perfect harmony with the divine commandments. There are two elements or forces engaged in the production of human affairs—the will of God and the volition of man. When these forces co-operate, we have an image of heaven. When the volition of man reacts against the will of God, we have an image of hell. When man resists or thwarts the Divine Will, nothing happens for the best, but everything for the worse or the worst. The quality of a result is to be determined by the predominance of the will of man or the will of God in its production.

The Lord always designs to give us the best. He would load us with blessings from the cradle to the grave; with health and joy and riches and felicity and long life. This is His will toward every human being. If it fails of consummation, it is because man, in the exercise of a free-agency inalienable and fundamental as the self-existence of God, has hindered it. Still God does not change His plan nor withdraw His love. After the commission of evil, as before it, the Lord's love flows in as warmly as at the first. But now the form is changed, and the result is changed also. We do not get the best good, but only the good possible under the circumstances; not the birthright blessing which was bestowed on Jacob, but only the second blessing which was given to Esau.

A man is bereft of his children by the malignant powers of hell, or by the spheres of infernal disorder and of evil. He is stricken to the earth by sorrow, as Paul was by the great light which arrested him on his journey. A gradual change comes over his spirit. He is weaned from the world, its follies and illusions and insane ambitions. His heart is humbled, and his nature softened and mellowed. He fixes his affections on spiritual things. His affliction is now regarded as a blessing in disguise; and God is supposed to have been the immediate cause of a calamity which was followed by so great a good. This, however, is a fallacy drawn from appearances.

God designed and willed a far greater blessing for that man than the one he attained. The pleasures, the duties, the responsibilities of paternity, enjoyed and exercised in perfect obedience to the commandments of God, would have developed in his soul a far richer and purer and brighter spirituality than that obtained by the ministration of sorrow. God's first and highest blessing, His will towards him, was prevented by evils hereditary or acquired; and shorn of much of its beauty and power, it fell upon the heart in a modified and inferior form.

The principle involved in this illustration is involved in all the events of life. After the self-inflicted wrong to our moral natures, called sin, and the inevitable calamities and trials it produces according to immutable laws, we are never the same beings we were before; we are not capable of receiving God's first, best, and highest gift which He had prepared for us, but only some secondary and inferior blessing. Even this blessing, however, is sometimes so great and glorious, that we feel that we have not suffered too much in its attainment. We are satisfied with what we call the chastenings of Providence.

The Lord's love never ceases to draw us from evil to good, and to bring or strive to bring spiritual treasures out of the darkest trials and keenest sufferings. There is some use or blessing in every thing, in heaven, earth and hell. Nothing exists or is done in the universe but by virtue of God's influent life, perverted as it may be when passing through evil forms. There is nothing so low, so base, so far from God, but has an element of use in it which connects it with the Centre of life and preserves it from annihilation.

The Lord governs the earth by influx through the hells as well as through the heavens. He turns the intense selfishness of man derived from hell into those vast schemes of labor, which build up a complicated civilization, with all its riches and splendors, its uses and pleasures, from a merely barbaric base. Self-love and love of the world, those master-springs of all our woes, are also the prime moving forces in every improvement in the arts and sciences, in manners, institutions, and governments. But who would say that the Lord made men selfish and grasping in order to bring about these great things?

The wildest storm will purify the atmosphere. The vilest offal will enrich the soil. From the direst poisons we extract the subtile essence which brings ease and health to the tortured frame. Idolatry preserved alive in the darkened soul some grateful idea of a God. Slavery had its uses and war its benefits. And while these things have been permitted in the providence of the Lord, who will affirm that He caused the tempest, the poisons, idolatry, slavery, and war, for the good which He foresaw would result from them?

The Lord gives us children for our sakes as well as theirs; for the world, for the church, for His heavenly kingdom; for a vast chain of beautiful and beneficent uses. He does not provide means for taking them from us, but all possible means to prevent them from being taken from us. He foresees that they will be taken away by the evil forces which disturb the peace and order of the moral world; and He provides new and wonderful blessings and uses in the place of those which He was ready at first to shower upon us, but which, through our own or others' sinfulness, He was prevented from doing.

With these qualifications as to the origin of sufferings, trials, and early death, we gratefully accept all the true and beautiful things which many charming writers have given us on the ministry of sorrow. The loss of children is especially calculated to subdue the heart to a heavenly tenderness, to enlarge and sweeten our sympathies with our fellow-men, to elevate and purify the affections, to wean the thoughts from the vain schemes of our earth-life, and to fix our attention, our hopes and our hearts on the spiritual world. We are likely to be better men and better citizens when some society of angels in heaven holds our children as hostages for our good behavior on earth.

It is needless to go over ground which has been so thoroughly canvassed by earnest and spiritual thinkers. It is our business rather to call attention to some of the peculiar blessings and manifest uses which may be, and so often are, derived from the death of children as viewed from the stand-point of a new Revelation.

The general advantages of an early demise to the children themselves can hardly be questioned. The terrible trials and sufferings and uncertainties of this life are all escaped. The final issue in eternal felicity is secured without the painful struggles which our adult spirits are compelled to undergo. It is no small comfort to the parental heart that the little one is safe from the world's storms, folded in the arms of the Good Shepherd; safe from the infestations of wicked spirits; safe from all evil things, present or future. The most unfortunate ones of earth no doubt enjoy a secret satisfaction in the thought, that their precious children have been led in flowery paths away from the dark road which has caused their own feet to bleed and their strength to faint.

The addition of a vast infantile population to the angelic world immeasurably increases the peace, beauty, joy, and power of heaven. Every soul added to an angelic society increases the general strength of affection and thought, the love, the wisdom, and the happiness of all the members. How glorious and beautiful must be those infantile heavens, created for children, in which the whole atmosphere sparkles with infinitesimal flowers and images of sporting infants! How wise and happy must they be who have them in charge! How sweet and holy must be the sphere which emanates from those infantile heavens to the entire spiritual kingdom of God!

This transcendent addition to the life and glory of heaven was not a part of the original design of God; but is an after-blessing, accruing from His divine mercy on the removal of children by evil spheres from the earthly life. No children are born in heaven. They are not needed there as essential parts of its organization. Man was designed to live to old age, and the work of our wicked Herods peoples the kingdom of Christ in a manner unforeseen by themselves.

Swedenborg describes with minuteness the very process by which sin brings about these calamities, which the Divine Providence immediately turns to such unexpected profit:

"As death [by disease] comes from no other source but sin, and sin includes every thing contrary to the divine order; it is therefore evil which closes the smallest and altogether invisible vessels [of the human body], of which the next greater vessels, also invisible, are composed; for the smallest and altogether invisible vessels are continued to a man's interiors. Hence comes the first and inmost obstruction, and hence the inmost vitiation of the blood. This vitiation, when it increases, causes disease, and at length death. But if man had lived the life of good, his interiors would be open to heaven and through heaven to the Lord. Thus the smallest and invisible vessels would be open also, and man would live without disease, and would only decrease to ultimate old age, until he became altogether an infant, but a wise one. When in such case the body could no longer minister to its internal man or spirit, he would pass without disease out of his terrestrial body into a body such as the angels have."

The sphere of infant life, sweet and powerful as it is on earth, becomes far sweeter and more powerful in heaven. It must flow down into our spirits with silent but incalculable might. If infants in heaven are sometimes sent to infants on earth, why may not our children be sent also to our bewildered and weary hearts on errands of comfort and mercy? Why may they not become ministering spirits to us? The influence of our children in heaven upon our lives on earth, cannot be estimated or accurately described; but it is a power in our hearts, soft, swift, and certain, like the "sweet influences" of Orion and the Pleiades.

The infantile heavens are of immense benefit in antagonizing and subduing the deepest and most terrible hells. Whilst living with us, infants are often the victims of diabolical spheres, against which they cannot defend themselves; for the order of influx is from the spiritual to the natural, from superior to inferior things, and not the contrary. When elevated, however, to the celestial heavens nearest the Lord, their sphere of innocence and peace flows downward into all the kingdoms beneath, and the Lord governs everything in heaven, earth, and hell by its power. The sphere of the celestial angels is similar, indeed the same, and fulfills the same uses; but the addition of the living and growing infantile sphere adds vastly to its power.

There are hells so terrible, so hideous, that they are shut up entirely by the Lord, like the mouths of the lions in the den with Daniel. They do not communicate with man, for their moral poison would as instantly corrupt the soul as the poison of the cobra destroys the body. These fearful monsters are probably held in control by the sphere of the infantile heaven, which being nearest the

Lord must antagonize that evil sphere which is farthest from Him.

Well may we be amazed at the offices and uses which our little ones may fill in the great economy of God. We are almost ready to think that these things were foreordained of the Lord, and to stand with abashed faces and silent lips in the presence of such beneficent designs. But our imaginations and our hearts do injustice to the love, wisdom, and power of the Divine Being, if we cannot conceive that far greater blessings and holier states would have been in store for us, had man not violated the moral order of the universe, brought sin into the world with all its woe, and created hell with all its horrors. Are we so overpowered by the three Sybilline Books we have obtained, that we forget the six others we might have possessed, but which we lost by our folly?

The chief good to be derived from evil is, that it shows us our own evil nature. Sin cannot be put away or renounced until it is discovered, and its nature and quality thoroughly understood. Self-knowledge is the great desideratum in morals; in the Christian it is synonymous with conviction of sin. The greatest crimes may even become blessings to the criminals, if they bring them to a clear perception of the unfathomable hells in their own hearts. The penitent thief, the self-abjuring murderer, is in a more salvable state than the complacent worldling or the self-righteous professor of religion who thinks himself better than other men.

The moral lesson involved in the death of infants and little children is of vast importance. It is a fearful index, a solemn reminder, not of what evil things we have done, but of what evil creatures we are. The moral story of intemperance is written in the life and death of the drunkard. Licentiousness stamps its terrible seal on the soul and body of its victim. This we can understand, for we see the connection here between cause and effect. But it takes the sufferings and death of little children to show us the hideous depravity of our hereditary nature; what evil forms we are, and how closely connected with hell, independently of any actual sin we may have ever committed.

It is not surprising that little children were so near and dear to the heart of Christ, when He saw them bearing, like Himself, the iniquities of others in their own bodies, yet without sin!

This fundamental perversion of our spiritual forms—this original sin, as it has been called, making it impossible for us to become good or wise of ourselves—is a cardinal doctrine of the Church, without a clear recognition of which, the Word of God and the mission of Christ will remain mysteries for ever. When we see the fearful workings of this hereditary nature, which connects us with all the hells, so painfully revealed in the sufferings and death of our beautiful and innocent children; and when we reflect that the same inexhaustible fountain of evil exists in our own souls, and that the most perfect self-culture can do nothing to suppress or destroy the plague; we will feel the want of that Great Saviour, who took upon himself our own hereditary nature and made it divine.

In contemplating the death of children, we should be led in an especial manner to hate, fear, and avoid sin; to humble ourselves with a sense of our organic, in-rooted, and terrible moral depravity; and to look to the Lord whose Divine Humanity is the life-bearing and power-giving medium between the Infinite and the finite.

Then there is great consolation in the thought that no calamity or sorrow, however grievous, is permitted to befall a single human being, which the Lord cannot and does not overrule for the highest ultimate good of that individual or of others. Evil spirits are not permitted to do any sort of evil, which cannot be so overruled. This reflection may, in some measure, assuage our bitterest griefs, and lighten our heaviest sorrows. Swedenborg says:

"The things which evil spirits are permitted to do, are only those which conduce to the emendation of man, of souls, and of spirits (other things are not permitted); all of which, even to the minutest particulars, the Lord so rules and governs, that there is not the slightest thing which they thus do as it were permissively, *which does not conduce to the good of many, thus to the good of the universe, and consequently of all.*"

"Infernal spirits strive with all their power to withdraw the good from heaven and plunge them into hell, since it is the very delight of their life to destroy any one as to his soul, thus to eternity; but not the smallest permission is given them by the Lord, except for the end that good may result therefrom. . . . In the whole spiritual world the end which proceeds from the Lord bears absolute sway; and this end is, that nothing whatever, not even the smallest circumstance, shall occur, but that good may come of it. Hence the Lord's kingdom is called a kingdom of ends and uses."

In accordance with this, the same enlightened author tells us why misfortunes are permitted to befall the righteous, and how, under the Divine Providence, they are rendered subservient to their spiritual welfare. Thus he says:

"I have conversed with angelic spirits concerning the misfortunes or distresses which befall the faithful, who, it is known, suffer in some cases as much as and even more than the wicked. The reason why some of them are thus let into temptations, was stated to be this: that they might not attribute goodness to themselves; for if they were exempted, they would attribute such exemption to their own goodness, and thus claim merit and righteousness to themselves. And that this may be prevented, misfortunes and distresses are permitted to come over them, that they may perish as to that life, and as to the inordinate love of wealth and possessions. But if they were not of such a character as to attribute goodness to themselves, they would be more frequently exempted from common misfortunes and distresses."

"They who put their trust in the Lord, continually receive good from Him; for whatsoever befalls them, whether it appear as prosperous or unprosperous, is still good, for it conduces as a means to their eternal felicity."

But the good to be derived from the death of

children, and indeed from all other calamities, will be greatly enhanced by tracing those evils boldly to their real and only source—the evil spheres of men and spirits. The Divine desire for their death being eliminated, the whole responsibility is thrown upon the Church in its greatest and least forms—the Church in the aggregate and in the individual. So long as we think that God has some sort of a causative share in all the events of life, the evil as well as the good, a strange apathy overcomes us, and we sink down in unthinking resignation to what we are taught to regard as His will. If God were, in our minds, freed from all complicity, direct or indirect, with evils or calamities, our awakened moral sense would seek to discover, by rigid self-examination, what share our own hearts and lives are daily contributing to the wars, slavery, pestilence, famine, catastrophes, intemperance, and social evils, which desolate the world.

The blessings sent us after afflictions will be more clearly seen and gratefully appreciated, when we realize fully the seven-fold light of the New Dispensation; when we can interpret the Word of God in a sense above that of the letter, judging not from the appearance, but judging righteous judgment; when we understand the laws and phenomena of the spiritual life; and when we see the Lord Jesus Christ in his Glorified Human Form as our Heavenly Father.

Infants on earth, angels in heaven, connecting one with the other,—our little ones have not lived or died in vain. They complete the golden circle of our spiritual life, leading from our weary and wounded hearts up through their shining and happy heavens to the great White Throne, and back again from the Lord himself through the diamond auras of their celestial sphere, down to the faith, the hope, the peace, the victory of the soul!

Glory and Dominion be unto the Lord Jesus Christ,
For ever and ever:
Who is, and Who was, and Who is to come:
The Almighty. Amen.

THE END.

www.ingramcontent.com/pod-product-compliance
Lightning Source LLC
LaVergne TN
LVHW020222110826
845151LV00003B/794

* 9 7 8 1 4 2 5 5 3 2 4 8 2 *